reviewing
pdf documents
in acrobat

Visual QuickProject Guide

by Donna Baker

**Peachpit
Press**

Visual QuickProject Guide
Reviewing PDF Documents in Acrobat
Donna Baker

Peachpit Press

1249 Eighth Street
Berkeley, CA 94710
510/524-2178
800/283-9444
510/524-2221 (fax)

Find us on the World Wide Web at: www.peachpit.com
To report errors, please send a note to errata@peachpit.com
Peachpit Press is a division of Pearson Education

Editor: Becky Morgan
Production Editor: Connie Jeung-Mills
Compositor: WolfsonDesign
Cover design: The Visual Group with Aren Howell
Cover production: WolfsonDesign
Cover photo credit: Dynamic Graphics
Interior design: Elizabeth Castro
Indexer: James Minkin

Notice of Rights

Notice of Liability

Trademarks

ISBN 0-321-32119-7

9 8 7 6 5 4 3 2 1

Printed and bound in the United States of America

For my friend Brooke Barker

Acknowledgements

For the past couple of years I have lived an exotic life vicariously through my dear friend Brooke. The project in this nifty little book is inspired by his adventures. I am indebted to our friend Maow who provided all the photos for the project under his formal name— Sakrapee Chalermsri.

การแสดงความขอบคุณ·มิตร

A special thank you to the terrific people at Peachpit, especially my editor, Becky Morgan. I enjoy the sense of collaboration and the enthusiasm you show in my work. It's inspiring!

Thanks as always to my dear hubby Terry, my daughter Erin, and my other girl Deena. And, of course, thanks to Tom Waits for growling truths into my brain.

contents

contents

introduction

The Visual QuickProject Guide that you hold in your hands offers a unique way to learn about new technologies. Instead of drowning you in theoretical possibilities and lengthy explanations, this Visual QuickProject Guide uses big, color illustrations coupled with clear, concise step-by-step instructions to show you how to complete one specific project in a matter of hours.

Our project in this book shows you how to create a PDF file, then conduct an email review in Acrobat 7 and Adobe Reader 7. As the review initiator, we'll use the Tracker in Acrobat 7 Professional to set up the review and invite recipients to comment on the project's content—the cover and Table of Contents pages for TravelASIA, a fictional travel magazine.

Then we'll put ourselves in the reviewer's place to see how to add comments to the file using Reader's Commenting and Drawing Markups tools. Once the comments are added, we send the comments back to the originator, and (back in the role of the initiator) integrate them into the original PDF file. We'll learn a number of ways to manage and work with the comments, including filtering, sorting, and printing a summary of the comments.

As you work through the project, you'll learn about different aspects of the review process and how they are managed in Acrobat. Although the content of this project is fictional, you'll be able to use what you learn in your own work, whether that involves circulating a document through your workgroup for commenting on the content, or creating a PDF slideshow that you add comments to before sharing with your friends, family, or colleagues.

what you'll create

Use a Stamp comment to define the document as a draft before sending it to review participants.

Allow recipients working with Adobe Reader 7, Acrobat 6, or Acrobat 7 to use the Commenting and Drawing Markups tools.

Use Text Edit commenting tools to define changes you'd like to make in the file's text.

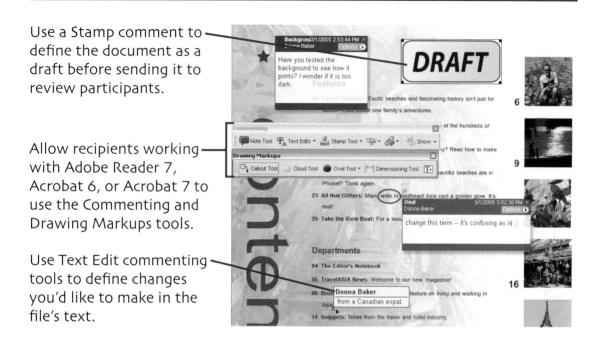

Import comments from a number of reviewers into the original document.

Reply to existing comments if further review cycles are required.

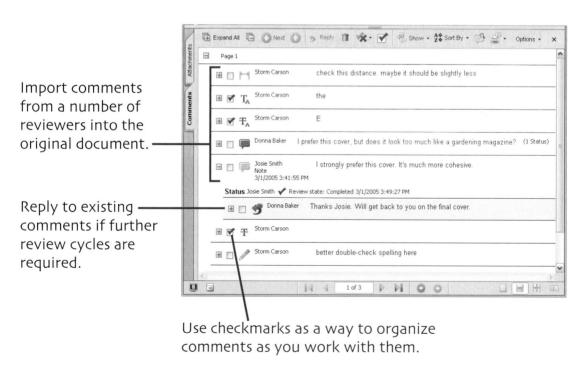

Use checkmarks as a way to organize comments as you work with them.

Create a report of the comments that you can save as a separate file, or print.

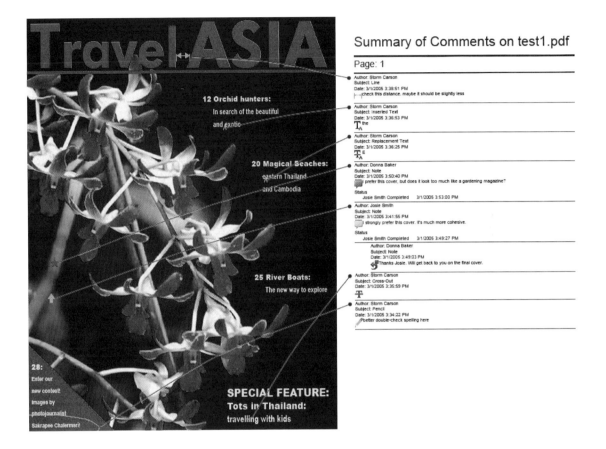

project steps

In this project, you get to be both the originator of a review and a participant (or reviewer). In this way, you see how the process works from both sides of the fence.

1 Create the PDF file as the originator. You work from within Acrobat and use the Create PDF from Multiple Files command to build the PDF file from a Word document and two image files.

2 Set up the review as the originator. Here's where you enable commenting tools for Adobe Reader users. The originator sends out the invitations (and reminders if need be!), and later collects and compiles comments from the reviewers.

3 Send the invitation. you can specify the people you want to invite to participate, and customize the email invitation.

4 In the role of reviewer, working with either Adobe Reader or Acrobat, add comments and drawing markups.

5 Send the information back to the originator. You can return either the entire PDF or just the comments.

6 Change back to your originator hat. As the reviewers return their comments to you, you import the comments back into your original PDF file.

7 Evaluate and process the comments. Sort the comments, reply or send them on to others as needed, and add checkmarks to keep track of your progress.

8 Create a report on the comments and actions taken.

9 Make edits to the text and images using Acrobat's TouchUp tools.

how this book works

The title of each section explains what is covered on that page or section.

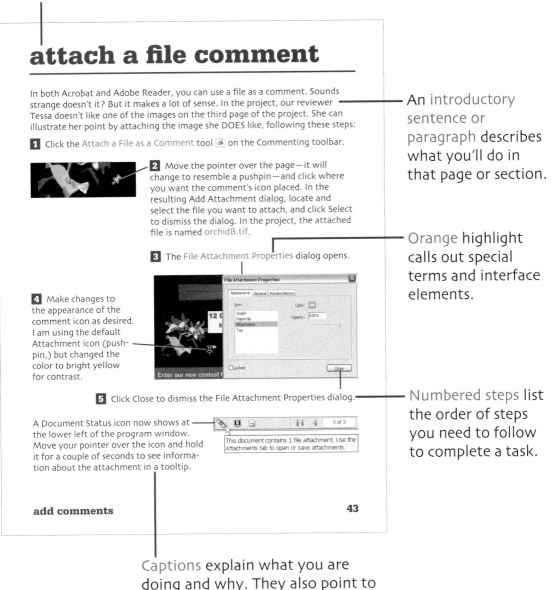

attach a file comment

In both Acrobat and Adobe Reader, you can use a file as a comment. Sounds strange doesn't it? But it makes a lot of sense. In the project, our reviewer Tessa doesn't like one of the images on the third page of the project. She can illustrate her point by attaching the image she DOES like, following these steps:

1 Click the Attach a File as a Comment tool 📎 on the Commenting toolbar.

An introductory sentence or paragraph describes what you'll do in that page or section.

2 Move the pointer over the page—it will change to resemble a pushpin—and click where you want the comment's icon placed. In the resulting Add Attachment dialog, locate and select the file you want to attach, and click Select to dismiss the dialog. In the project, the attached file is named orchidB.tif.

3 The File Attachment Properties dialog opens.

Orange highlight calls out special terms and interface elements.

4 Make changes to the appearance of the comment icon as desired. I am using the default Attachment icon (push-pin,) but changed the color to bright yellow for contrast.

5 Click Close to dismiss the File Attachment Properties dialog.

Numbered steps list the order of steps you need to follow to complete a task.

A Document Status icon now shows at the lower left of the program window. Move your pointer over the icon and hold it for a couple of seconds to see information about the attachment in a tooltip.

add comments 43

Captions explain what you are doing and why. They also point to areas of the Acrobat interface.

how this book works (cont.)

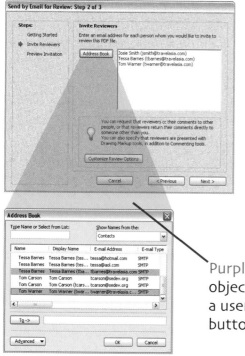

Dotted arrows show interactive movement such as dragging a comment to a new location

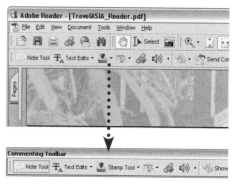

Purple tint connecting two objects shows the effect of a user action, like clicking a button to open a dialog.

The extra bits section at the end of each chapter contains additional tips and tricks that you might like to know—but that aren't absolutely necessary for conducting a review or processing comments.

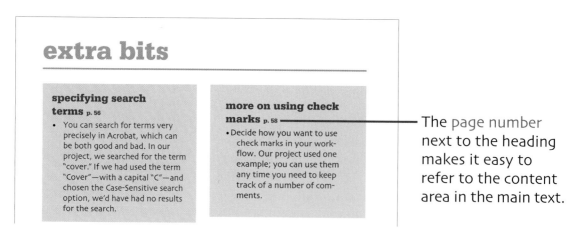

extra bits

specifying search terms p. 56

- You can search for terms very precisely in Acrobat, which can be both good and bad. In our project, we searched for the term "cover." If we had used the term "Cover"—with a capital "C"—and chosen the Case-Sensitive search option, we'd have had no results for the search.

more on using check marks p. 58

- Decide how you want to use check marks in your workflow. Our project used one example; you can use them any time you need to keep track of a number of comments.

The page number next to the heading makes it easy to refer to the content area in the main text.

the web site

You can find this book's companion Web site at
http://www.donnabaker.ca/acro7_vqp.html.

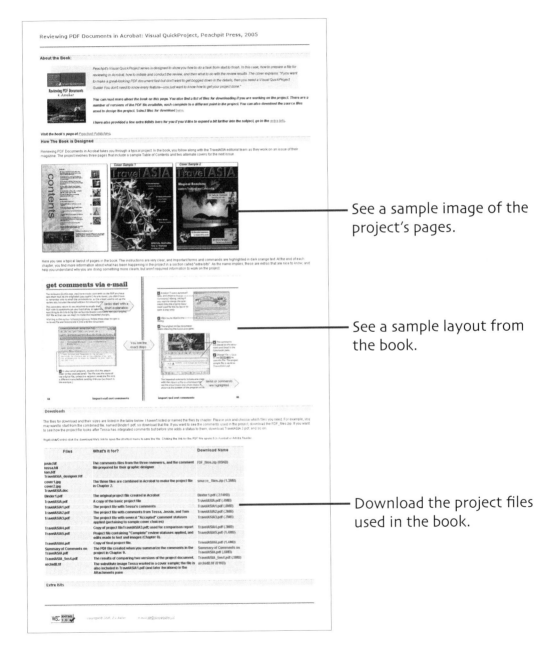

See a sample image of the project's pages.

See a sample layout from the book.

Download the project files used in the book.

useful tools

To work with commenting and reviewing processes, you need Acrobat 7, either Professional or Standard edition. I used Acrobat 7 Professional to create the book's project because only Professional allows you to specify that Adobe Reader users can also participate in the review.

Adding comments can be done in Acrobat 6, Acrobat 7, or Adobe Reader 7. If you want to see how the process works in Adobe Reader, you'll have to install that program separately from Adobe Acrobat.

The project shows how to conduct an e-mail-based review, which means, of course, that you need an e-mail program. I used Microsoft Outlook in the project, but any e-mail program will work as well.

A bonus project available from the book's Web site shows you to return comments from Acrobat to a source Word document. This integration process only works in Word for Windows, version 2002 and newer.

the next step

While this Visual QuickProject Guide will walk you through all of the steps required to start and manage a review, as well as to add, import, and work with comments, there is so much more to learn about Acrobat. After you complete this project, consider picking up one of my other books on Acrobat, both published by Adobe Press, for an in-depth, handy reference.

Adobe Acrobat 7 Tips and Tricks: The 150 Best shows you many ways to work with Acrobat's tools and processes that save time and effort. Numerous examples show how the tips are applied in a practical way.

the next step (cont.)

If you are the type of person that learns best by doing, take a look at Adobe Acrobat 7 in the Office. This is a project-based book that shows you how to use Acrobat's many features to build 13 separate projects—ranging from interactive forms, to a map containing pop-ups, to a series of projects on developing an interactive form. The book's companion Web site offers four additional projects, all the files used in the book and bonus projects, as well as more customizations and activities.

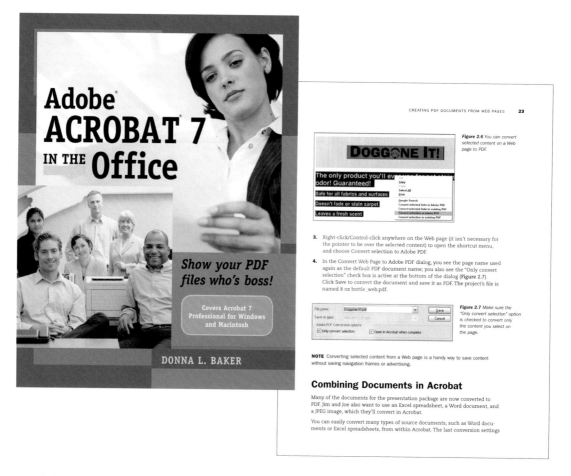

Both books give you clear examples, concise, step-by-step instructions, and many helpful tips to help you become an efficient Acrobat user.

1. explore acrobat 7

Before you get started on the document review project, you need to know how to make your way around the programs you'll be working with in this book, Acrobat 7 and Adobe Reader 7. The Windows and Mac versions of the programs are so similar that instructions for one version of the programs usually work for the other.

Start Acrobat 7 to take a look around. In Windows, click Start on the Status bar, choose Programs, then choose Adobe, and finally choose Acrobat 7.

On the Mac, open the Applications folder, then open the Adobe folder, and double-click the Acrobat 7 icon.

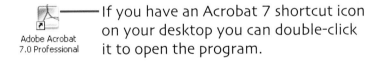

If you have an Acrobat 7 shortcut icon on your desktop you can double-click it to open the program.

Adobe Acrobat
7.0 Professional

In this chapter, you see what makes up Acrobat 7 Professional.

the acrobat 7 layout

Adobe Acrobat 7 Standard and Professional display the same components in the program window. In this image, a document is shown open in Acrobat 7 Professional for Windows.

The Basic toolbar contains the two tools you'll use the most— the Hand tool and the Select tool.

The Menu bar displays across the top of the program.

The File toolbar has commands for opening, searching, and organizing PDF files.

The Task Buttons each contain related commands for performing a specific type of work.

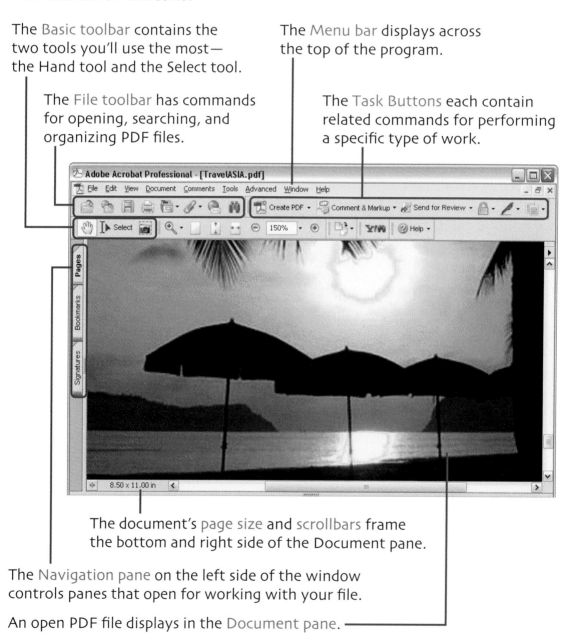

The document's page size and scrollbars frame the bottom and right side of the Document pane.

The Navigation pane on the left side of the window controls panes that open for working with your file.

An open PDF file displays in the Document pane.

The Comments pane is the happening place in this project!
It opens horizontally across the program window.

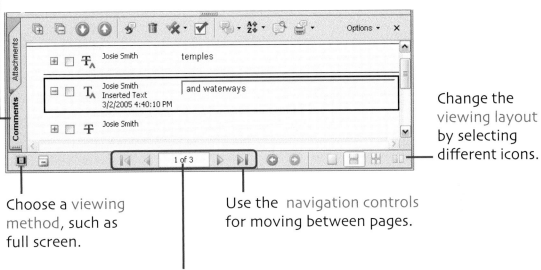

Change the viewing layout by selecting different icons.

Choose a viewing method, such as full screen.

Use the navigation controls for moving between pages.

At the bottom of the program window you see information about the document's page numbers.

The How To window links to the Help files and offers explanations of common tasks.

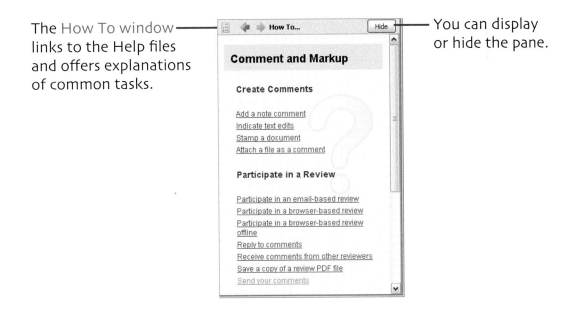

You can display or hide the pane.

toolbars and buttons

Acrobat offers a fair number of toolbars. You can modify the appearance and display of the toolbars in the program, but you can't remove or add commands on the existing toolbars.

A toolbar icon with a pull-down arrow to the right indicates that a subtoolbar is available.

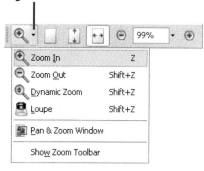

Move your pointer over the hatched line at the left edge of a toolbar to see the toolbar's name in a tooltip.

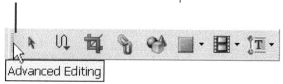

Task buttons are different from toolbars in that each button contains a number of similar commands for performing a type of task, rather than different related tools.

extra bits

keeping your place p. 2

- Working with a small document, it isn't very hard to keep track of where you are in a file; you can close and reopen the document and still easily find your place. On the other hand, if you are working with a monstrous file, set a preference to automatically open the file at the page you left off last. Choose Edit > Preferences (Acrobat > Preferences on Mac) and click the Startup category in the left column to display the Startup Preferences. Click the Reopen Documents to Last Viewed Page pull-down arrow and choose All Files. Now when you reopen a file, you see the last page you viewed.

- Setting the preference to show you the last page you viewed works only during a single session. If you close and reopen Acrobat, you won't open at the last location you worked on.

special features p. 2

- Acrobat tells you when you open a document containing special features. An icon shows at the left of the status bar when your file contains features such as file attachments ✎, security such as certification or signatures ⚷✒, or layers 📚.

using locked toolbars p. 4

- If you are working with a particular group of tasks, like commenting, you work with the same toolbars for some time. Save yourself time in looking for tools by locking the toolbar in a configuration you like. Right-click/Ctrl-click the toolbar well and choose Lock Toolbars from the shortcut menu. The separator bars disappear between the different toolbars. In the project, you might find it helpful to have the Commenting and Drawing Markups toolbars locked together and docked in the toolbar area.

- When a toolbar is locked, you can't drag it from the toolbar area and float it over the program window, nor can you drag a floating toolbar to join with the other toolbars.

extra bits

taming toolbars p. 4

- If you have too many toolbars open and want to simplify things quickly, right-click/Ctrl-click the toolbar well and choose Reset Toolbars.

one-click commands p. 4

- In Acrobat 7, when you move your pointer over a tool's icon on a toolbar, you sometimes see an initial following its name.

  This initial is the shortcut key that you can press to activate the tool. In order to get the one-click action, you need to specify a preference—choose Edit > Preferences (Acrobat > Preferences on Mac) and click the General category in the left column to display the General Preferences. Click the Use single-key accelerators to access tools check box.

2. creating pdf files

Before you can review a PDF document, you need the PDF file itself! This project uses a Table of Contents created as a Word document and two alternate magazine cover images that were created as Photoshop images.

Although many programs, such as those in Microsoft Office, include ways to create PDF files, the method you choose often depends on your workflow—the application you are currently working with and how you intend to work with the PDF file. Our project is simple, so we'll use tools inside Acrobat itself—it's the coolest way to go.

You create a PDF file using Acrobat's settings from a number of different locations on your computer. The file in our project is intended for online use, meaning it is designed for reading and working with onscreen as opposed to being printed. Acrobat offers different groups of settings called conversion settings that you choose to create a PDF file for a specific purpose. The different settings are saved on your computer as joboptions files, and describe how objects such as images and fonts are managed in the PDF file. Choosing the online settings creates the smallest file size, which is important when emailing a PDF file, as we will do later in the project.

After checking the original document in Word, you work for the rest of the chapter (and the book!) in Acrobat. You set the conversion settings for both the Word and image files in Acrobat's Preferences dialog. Then you use one of Acrobat's handy PDF creation methods to convert the set of three files for the project to a single PDF file called a binder.

check the text file

First, take a minute and check the Word file's contents. Essentially, check the document the same way you would before printing. Be sure the content is organized correctly, the text is understandable, sentence structure is consistent, and so on.

Although you can make editing changes in Acrobat (like those you'll learn about in Chapter 9), it's simpler to make changes in the source file. Also, if you need to work with the Word document at a later time, its contents will be correct.

Check spelling and grammar

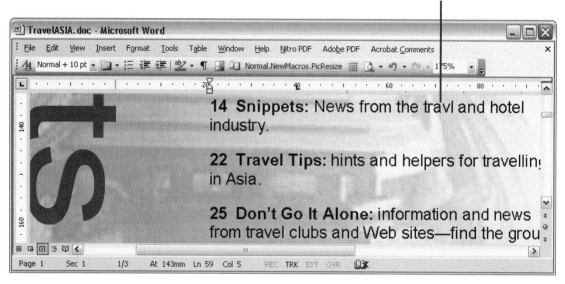

In some cases, it's necessary to check fonts and images prior to converting the file. Since our project is intended for online use, we won't have any fonts embedded, or included within the file's code. Nor do we have any particular image resolution or compression issues as images are automatically compressed for viewing online.

Once the file is checked, save it and close Word.

pick conversion method

Now open Acrobat; we are going to convert both the document and the image files to PDF together in Acrobat to use for the review.

Before converting files, check Acrobat's preferences and make changes if needed. The program offers a number of choices for converting both text and image files. Since Acrobat uses the last selected formats chosen in the text and image conversion settings, you should always check the settings first before converting files.

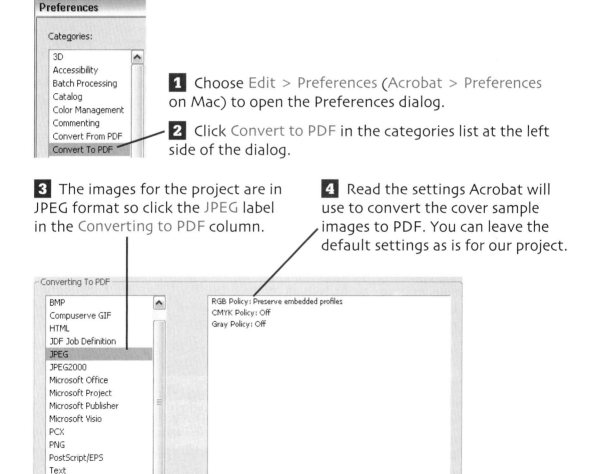

1 Choose Edit > Preferences (Acrobat > Preferences on Mac) to open the Preferences dialog.

2 Click Convert to PDF in the categories list at the left side of the dialog.

3 The images for the project are in JPEG format so click the JPEG label in the Converting to PDF column.

4 Read the settings Acrobat will use to convert the cover sample images to PDF. You can leave the default settings as is for our project.

pick conversion method

5 Click Microsoft Office in the
Converting to PDF column.

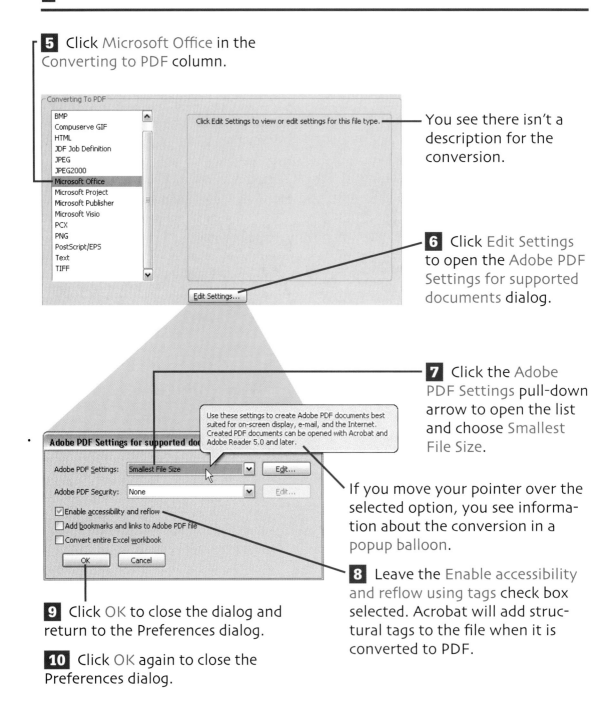

You see there isn't a
description for the
conversion.

6 Click Edit Settings
to open the Adobe PDF
Settings for supported
documents dialog.

7 Click the Adobe
PDF Settings pull-down
arrow to open the list
and choose Smallest
File Size.

If you move your pointer over the
selected option, you see information about the conversion in a
popup balloon.

8 Leave the Enable accessibility
and reflow using tags check box
selected. Acrobat will add struc-
tural tags to the file when it is
converted to PDF.

9 Click OK to close the dialog and
return to the Preferences dialog.

10 Click OK again to close the
Preferences dialog.

create the pdf file

Now that your settings are selected, it's time to choose the files to use for the project's PDF file. We are creating the PDF file using one of Acrobat's task features.

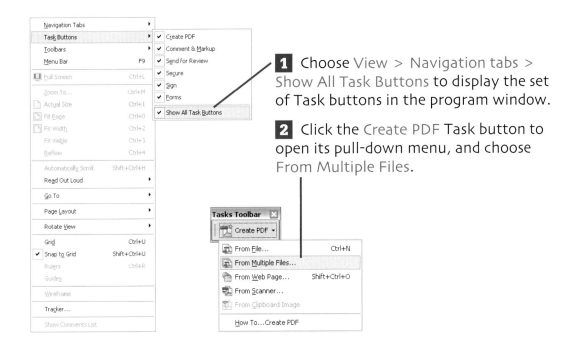

1 Choose View > Navigation tabs > Show All Task Buttons to display the set of Task buttons in the program window.

2 Click the Create PDF Task button to open its pull-down menu, and choose From Multiple Files.

3 When the Create PDF from Multiple Documents dialog opens, click Browse in the Add Files section of the dialog.

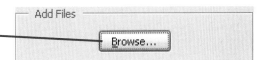

create the pdf file (cont.)

4 In the Open dialog, browse to the location where you have stored the files and select them. Ctrl/⌘-click to select the three files for the project—TravelASIA.doc, cover1.jpg, and cover2.jpg.

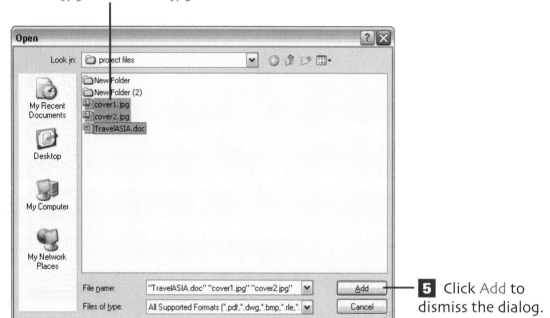

5 Click Add to dismiss the dialog.

6 The three files appear in the Create PDF dialog. To reorder the list of files, click the file's name to select it, and then click Move Up or Move Down as required.

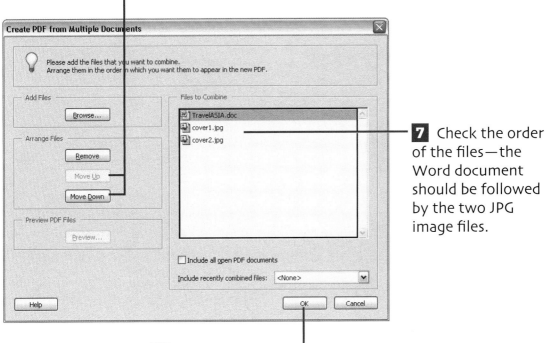

7 Check the order of the files—the Word document should be followed by the two JPG image files.

8 Click OK to dismiss the dialog and begin the conversion process.

create the pdf file (cont.)

9 Acrobat opens a series of progress information dialogs as the files are converted to PDF.

10 When the files are processed, the information dialogs close and the Save As dialog opens. You see Acrobat has named the file Binder1.pdf by default. You can use this name, or type a different name.

11 Choose the storage location for the file.

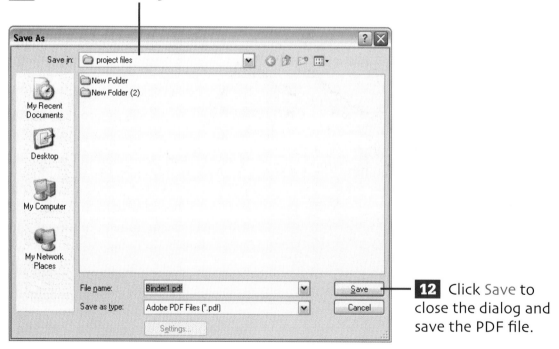

12 Click Save to close the dialog and save the PDF file.

extra bits

pdf conversion options p. 10

- The four PDF conversion options used most often are:

- Standard—This is the PDFMaker default, used for basic business documents. The Standard settings print at a resolution of 600 dpi.

- High Quality—The High Quality print settings use higher image resolutions, and print at 2400 dpi. There is only a limited amount of information about the document's fonts.

- Press—Press settings are used for for high-end print production, such as image setters, and print at a high resolution. All the information about the document and its fonts are included in the PDF file.

- Smallest File Size—The smaller the file, the easier it is to email or download. The Smallest File Size settings compress images and decrease their resolution. Fonts are not embedded.

shared conversion settings p. 10

- The conversion settings are shared throughout your system. The same conversion choices you selected in the Acrobat preferences are also used by Acrobat's PDFMakers, in Acrobat Distiller, in the Adobe PDF (Adobe PDF 7.0) printer driver, and other programs that export PDF files directly such as Adobe Creative Suite products.

project files p. 11

- You can download the source files used in the project from the book's Web site.

- The project files are:TravelASIA. doc, cover1.jpg, and cover2.jpg

- The Web site also includes a copy of the binder file created in this chapter named Binder1.pdf; the same name used if you convert the files in Acrobat yourself.

extra bits

about source programs p. 11

- Although it appears that Acrobat is converting your file internally, the program actually uses the PDFMaker it installs into other programs to do the conversions.

- This means that Acrobat can't create a PDF file from a source file unless the source program is available on your computer. For example, if you want to convert an Access database file to PDF, you must have Access on your computer.

3. setting up a review

In this chapter, you are the gal (or man) in charge. Your mission is to get the review underway, and Acrobat is here to help you. We want our recipients who are using Adobe Reader 7 to participate in the review. To do this, they need a special enabled version of the file that can only be prepared in Acrobat 7 Professional. Although you can start a review using Acrobat 7 Standard, you can't provide additional rights to users working with Adobe Reader, as I intend to do in this project.

The first part of the process is to open the file to work with, and then start the actual review cycle. The person (you!) who starts the review is called the originator or initiator—we'll use both terms in the project.

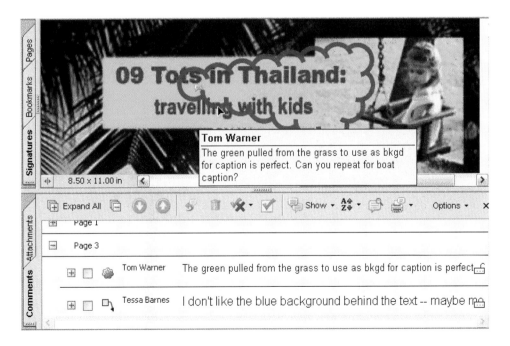

review with the wizard

Although you can send a PDF file to anyone by email and have them add comments (using Acrobat, not Reader), it's easier and more efficient to use the provided review wizard. The advantage of the wizard is that it keeps a record of the review in Acrobat's Tracker window. The Tracker can automatically send emails and receive returned comments, saving a lot of time over the course of the project.

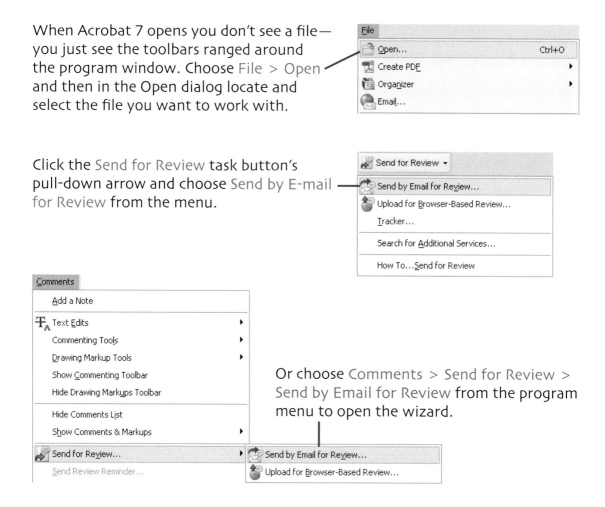

When Acrobat 7 opens you don't see a file—you just see the toolbars ranged around the program window. Choose File > Open and then in the Open dialog locate and select the file you want to work with.

Click the Send for Review task button's pull-down arrow and choose Send by E-mail for Review from the menu.

Or choose Comments > Send for Review > Send by Email for Review from the program menu to open the wizard.

select a review file

In the Send by Email for Review wizard you see
there are three steps listed at the left of the dialog.

The name of the dialog changes
as you move through the wizard.

Send by Email for Review: Step 1 of 3

Steps:
- ➡ Getting Started
- Invite Reviewers
- Preview Invitation

Getting Started: Initiating an Email-Based Review

Acrobat 7.0 Professional allows you to send PDFs by email for review
and helps you to track and aggregate the comments you receive from
reviewers.

- Recipients of the file receive tools and instructions to assist them in
  reviewing and commenting on the PDF.

- Recipients are assisted in sending their comments back to you via email.
  You will be given the option to merge comments back onto your copy of
  the PDF as you receive them.

- Anyone can participate! Anyone with the Free Adobe Reader 7.0 or
  later, or with Acrobat 6.0 or later, can review and comment on your
  PDF.

Specify a PDF file to Send by Email for Review:

TravelASIA.pdf ▼   Browse...

Cancel   < Previous   Next >

Click the pull-down arrow on
the Step 1 pane and choose
an open document.

Click Next.

invite recipients

The second step involves two processes. First, we'll specify the review recipients' email addresses; then we'll customize the settings. First things first...

On the Step 2 pane, click in the Invite Reviewers box and type the recipients' email addresses.

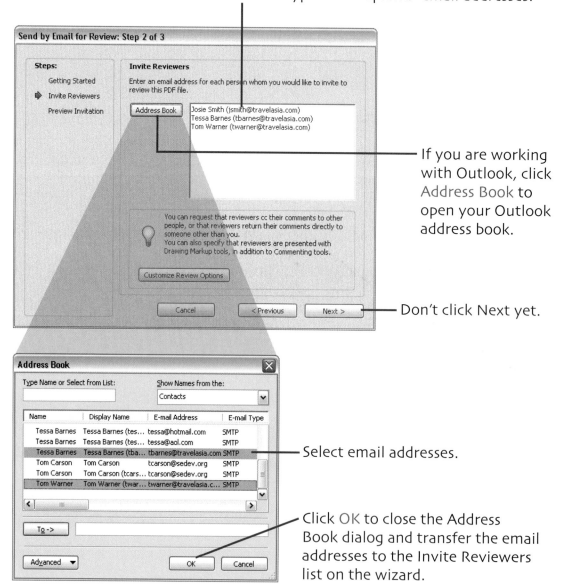

If you are working with Outlook, click Address Book to open your Outlook address book.

Don't click Next yet.

Select email addresses.

Click OK to close the Address Book dialog and transfer the email addresses to the Invite Reviewers list on the wizard.

20   **setting up a review**

customize the review

When you are setting up an email review you can customize the options available for your reviewers. On the second pane of the Send by Email for Review wizard, click Customize Review Options.

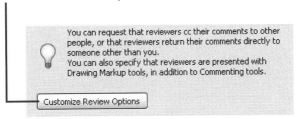

Choose from several customization options in the Review Options dialog.

Suppose you are setting up the review, but want the results returned to your assistant—in that case, specify the comments should be sent to an email address other than yours.

Click the Address Book button to select an address from your Outlook Address Book.

Include special commenting tools called Drawing Markups for your reviewers to use.

Most important for this project —allow reviewers using Adobe Reader 7 to participate.

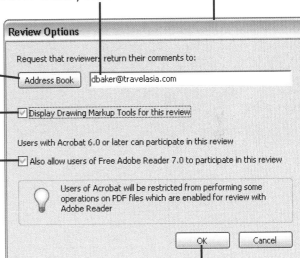

When you have finished, click OK to close the dialog and return to the wizard.

Now click Next in the wizard to go to the third, and final pane.

send review invitations

On the Step 3 pane, you get to preview the contents of the invitation that is sent to the reviewers.

You can easily replace the text in the default message, as I have done. Click in the message and select and replace the text as desired. For example, specify the due date in the subject line, such as: "Due back by 6/12: Table of Contents and Cover Samples."

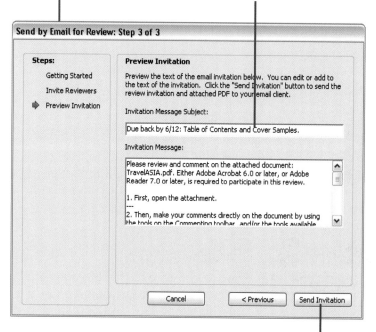

When you are finished, click Send Invitation to close the wizard and start the review email on its way.

An Outgoing Message Notification information dialog opens explaining what happens next. The email may be sent automatically, or you may need to move through dialogs approving the mail process, depending on your email program's security settings.

Outgoing Message Notification

An email message with TravelASIA.pdf attached has been given to your default email application. If your email application is configured to send email automatically on a schedule, the email will be sent automatically.

If not, you will need to send the message manually.

☐ Don't show again   OK ────── Click OK to dismiss the dialog.

You will see the outgoing email in your email program, listing the names of the recipients you added, as well as the message you used.

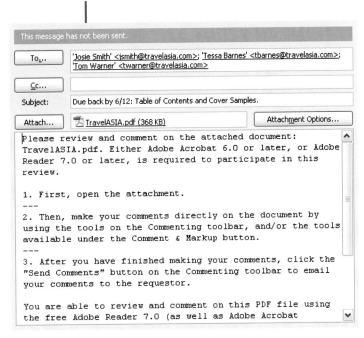

This message has not been sent.

To:.. | 'Josie Smith' <jsmith@travelasia.com>; 'Tessa Barnes' <tbarnes@travelasia.com>; 'Tom Warner' <twarner@travelasia.com>

Cc... |

Subject: | Due back by 6/12: Table of Contents and Cover Samples.

Attach... | TravelASIA.pdf (368 KB) | Attachment Options...

Please review and comment on the attached document: TravelASIA.pdf. Either Adobe Acrobat 6.0 or later, or Adobe Reader 7.0 or later, is required to participate in this review.

1. First, open the attachment.
---
2. Then, make your comments directly on the document by using the tools on the Commenting toolbar, and/or the tools available under the Comment & Markup button.
---
3. After you have finished making your comments, click the "Send Comments" button on the Commenting toolbar to email your comments to the requestor.

You are able to review and comment on this PDF file using the free Adobe Reader 7.0 (as well as Adobe Acrobat

check the review

Once the email is on its way, your review is started. You can see the new review, along with any other reviews you are involved with, in Acrobat's Tracker. Choose Comments > Tracker, or click the Send for Review Task button and choose Tracker from its menu. The Tracker opens as a separate window.

The details of the review are shown in the right pane of the Tracker window. You see the name of the review, as well as the date it was started, and the storage location for the review document. You'll also see a list of review participants that are active hyperlinks—click a name of a participant to open an email window addressed to the selected reviewer.

Click the name of the review you want to check on.

```
Tracker                                                              _ □ ✕

Open   Expand   Collapse   Services ▾   New Folder...   Remove   Manage ▾

⊟ 🗐 My Reviews                     TravelASIA.pdf Review
    📄 TravelASIA.pdf
    📄 1202.pdf                     Type: Email-Based Review
    📄 Product Manual.pdf           Sent on: 3/15/2005 1:38:50 PM
    📄 contract_sign.pdf            Location: C:\aa_vqp\project files\New Folder\TravelASIA.pdf
  📄 Participant Reviews
  📄 Offline Documents              Sent to:

                                      • Josie Smith (jsmith@travelasia.com)
                                      • Tessa Barnes (tbarnes@travelasia.com)
                                      • Tom Warner (twarner@travelasia.com)
```

Click the (+) to the left of My Reviews in the left column of the Tracker. The (+) changes to (-), and the list of active reviews displays below the heading.

extra bits

check and double-check p. 18

- Make sure to carefully check the content of the document before starting a review. There is nothing more annoying than circulating a document for review, and then receiving comments from all your reviewers telling you about the typo at the top of page 37. Not only is reading and rereading about your typo annoying, it also takes time for each reviewer to make the same comment.

email issues p. 20

- The Send by Email for Review dialog uses a specific filter on the email name you enter. If your email address doesn't end in a three-letter suffix—.com, .net, and so on—you may receive an error. To avoid this, in the Identity panel of the Preferences dialog box, type your email address in the email address field, and then click OK.

- You don't have to worry about your recipients' email addresses, though, as the filter isn't applied to recipients.

other ways to open files p. 19

- You can click the Open icon on the File toolbar ⊟ to display an Open dialog; locate and select the file you want to use.

- You can choose File > Open and then select the file from the list of recently-used documents at the bottom of the File menu if you have worked with it recently.

- You can also use Acrobat's History feature to find your file. Choose File > History to open the list of time frames. Click the time frame closest to the date you last worked with the file, and then select the file from the list.

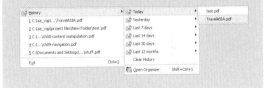

hiding prompts p. 22

- When you are sending out the invitations to a review, you receive an Outgoing Message Notification information dialog. Click Don't show again if you like—once you've started a few review cycles, you certainly know how to send the email!

extra bits

power selections p. 20

- It's common to work with the same reviewers repeatedly as part of your regular workflow. If you are using Outlook, use a Distribution List so you won't have to select individual names each time you need to send a document for review.

- If you regularly conduct reviews with different groups of people, create a separate Distribution List for each type of review. Make sure to name the lists using a descriptive name, such as "Mag Review".

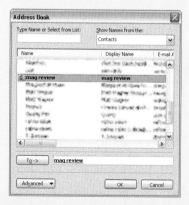

effects of enabling a file p. 21

- When you enable a document in Acrobat 7 to allow Adobe Reader 7 users to use Commenting tools, some features in Acrobat 7 are restricted, such as inserting and deleting pages, changing content using TouchUp tools, , signing the document, and filling form fields.

browser-based reviews p. 24

- In addition to conducting reviews via email, you can also send files to reviewers over the Internet. In some situations, this has distinct advantages over working through email.

- A browser-based review lets you work anytime, anywhere, as long as you can access files uploaded to a server folder by Internet. Now you can have access to more of your work files while on vacation!

- A browser-based review can be used in Windows, and is supported on the Mac using Safari 1.3, and Mac OS 10.3.x. You can choose and configure a server for conducting the review either through the program's preferences or on a file-by-file basis.

- Click the Send for Review task button's pull-down arrow and choose Upload for Browser-Based Review to open a wizard very similar to the Send by Email for Review wizard. The only difference is that you must select a server folder.

4. opening a file for review

There are two sides to a review; you've seen how to work as the initiator, or originator of the review, and how to configure the file and send out the invitations. In this next part of the project you are going to become somebody else. It's just for a while, and it won't hurt a bit!

In this chapter, you will see how to open and look at the project file in Adobe Reader 7—you can also use the file in Acrobat 6 or 7. In order for a file to be commented on in Adobe Reader, it must be enabled, that is, special rights must be granted by the originator of the review to allow the extra tools and features to be available in Adobe Reader. Rights are enabled for an individual file, not for the entire program. Our project file was enabled for Adobe Reader in the previous chapter.

open review document

The review originator has sent reviewers an email with the PDF file attached.

The email message arrives in your Inbox. You can open the file either by double-clicking the attachment in your email program, or by saving it to your hard drive and then opening it.

To open the file in Adobe Reader, first open the program and then choose File > Open.

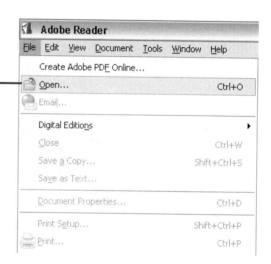

In the Open dialog box, locate and select the project file and click Open. When the file opens, you see a number of extra features:

The Document Message Bar tells you that you can use Commenting tools, and explains how to proceed through the review.

A Comment & Markup Task button appears on the Adobe Reader toolbar.

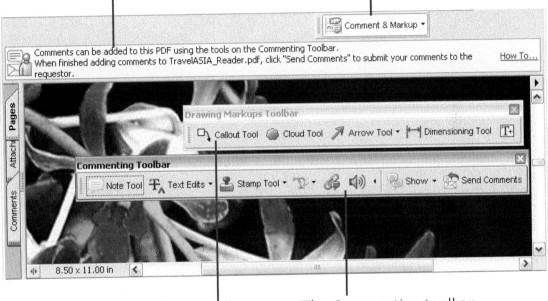

The Drawing Markups toolbar opens overlaying the file.

The Commenting toolbar opens overlaying the file.

open review document

The Comments tab is included in the Navigation tabs at the left of the program window.

The Comments pane lists any comments added to the file.

Select the tab to open and collapse the Comments pane.

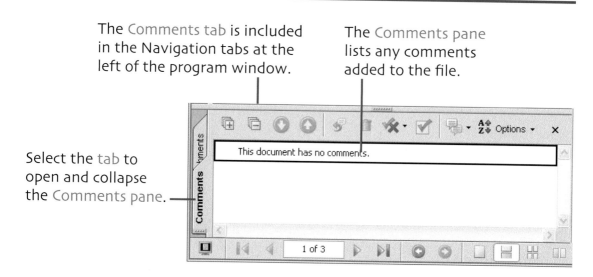

This document has no comments.

1 of 3

Click Hide to close the How To window.

The How To window, on the right side of the window, shows information about working in a review, describing how to participate. This is the first panel; scroll down for more.

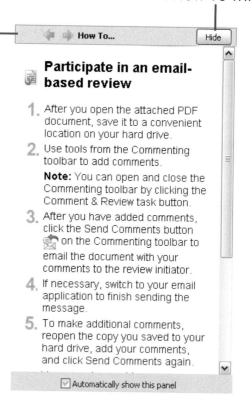

How To...   Hide

Participate in an email-based review

1. After you open the attached PDF document, save it to a convenient location on your hard drive.

2. Use tools from the Commenting toolbar to add comments.

   Note: You can open and close the Commenting toolbar by clicking the Comment & Review task button.

3. After you have added comments, click the Send Comments button on the Commenting toolbar to email the document with your comments to the review initiator.

4. If necessary, switch to your email application to finish sending the message.

5. To make additional comments, reopen the copy you saved to your hard drive, add your comments, and click Send Comments again.

☑ Automatically show this panel

manage reader's window

There isn't a lot of extra space on a computer screen—wading through unnecessary tools and windows can make it impossible to see the task at hand. As you're getting ready to start working on the file, remember to move toolbars and windows out of your way whenever you can to make it easier to read your document.

Drag the Commenting and Drawing Markups toolbars to the toolbar area of the program to dock them.

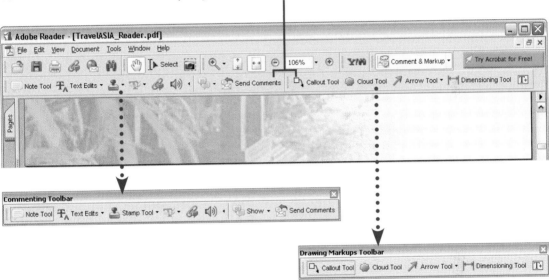

manage reader's window

If you close the toolbars by mistake, don't fret. Since the file is enabled in Adobe Reader, the toolbars are now included in the program. Choose View > Toolbars, and select the toolbar you'd like to open.

opening a file for review

how to how to

The How To window displays in a pane at the right side of the program window. You can drag the pane wider, but you can't make it narrower than the default width. There are a few ways to get more information to help with your review, using different areas of Adobe Reader 7:

When the How To window is closed, click How To on the Document Message Bar to reopen the window's pane.

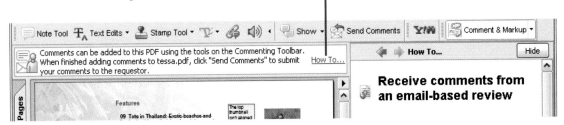

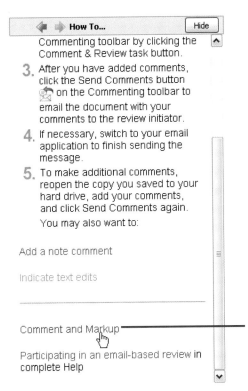

Scroll down and click Comment and Markup at the bottom of the How To window's default list of topics.

how to how to (cont.)

A listing of Help topics displays on everything you need to know about adding comments to a file.

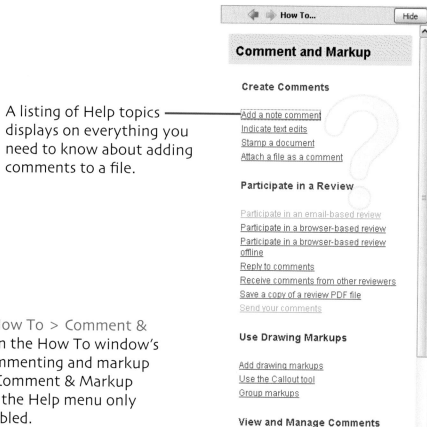

Choose Help > How To > Comment & Markup to reopen the How To window's default list of commenting and markup help topics. The Comment & Markup listing appears in the Help menu only when a file is enabled.

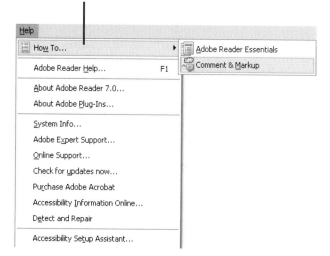

extra bits

how the review file looks in acrobat p. 28

- Although in this chapter I am showing how to review the project file in Adobe Reader, you can certainly work with the file in Acrobat! If you do open a document that's been enabled for use in Adobe Reader, you'll see a Document Status dialog when you first open the program. Click OK to dismiss the dialog.

- While the enabled document is open, you see a Document Status icon on the bottom left of the program window. Move your pointer over the icon to read a tooltip describing what has been changed in the file.

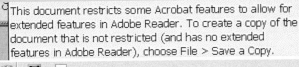

document message bar p. 31

- Once you have opened a file in Adobe Reader and understand how to work with its review features, you don't have to keep the Document Message Bar visible. Free up a bit of screen real estate by closing it. Move your pointer over the bottom edge of the message bar area. When you see the pointer change to double arrows and horizontal lines, drag upward to collapse the Document Message Bar area.

- If you want to see the message again, or to use the How To link, move your pointer over the upper edge of the Document pane. Again, you'll see the pointer change to the double arrows and lines. This time, drag downward. Release the mouse and the message bar is shown again.

extra bits

hiding help p. 33

- When you have worked with Acrobat or Adobe Reader for a while, you don't need to see the How To window each time you open a file for reviewing. Look for the check box below the How To window that reads "Automatically show this panel" and uncheck the check box. The next time you open a review file, you won't have to waste an extra mouse click hiding the How To window.

☑ Automatically show this panel

opening a file for review

5. add comments

You've received the email from the originator, and opened the file for review in Adobe Reader 7.Now it's time to to add some comments to the TravelASIA magazine cover samples and table of contents.

Acrobat includes a wide range of comment types. I'm going to show you how to add comments as one of the magazine content reviewers, working with both the Commenting and the Drawing Markups toolbars, as well as the Comments pane.

When you have seen how to add and configure different types of comments, you'll see how to send them back to the originator of the review. The comments shown in the project are available in FDF format from the book's Web site. There are three other FDF files containing reviewers' comments that you can practice with.

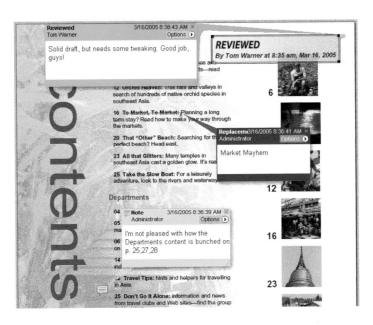

place a note comment

The most common type of comment is a note, which can be used to comment on either text or images. The note identifies its author and the time and date it was added to the file. You can include as much text as you'd like in a note; scroll bars will appear in the text box to accomodate lengthy comments.

Follow these steps to add a Note comment:

1 Click the Note tool ▦ on the Commenting toolbar.

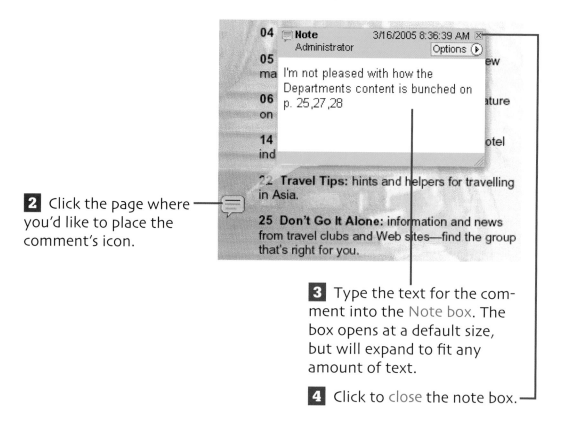

2 Click the page where you'd like to place the comment's icon.

3 Type the text for the comment into the Note box. The box opens at a default size, but will expand to fit any amount of text.

4 Click to close the note box.

change note appearance

You can change a number of aspects of a comment's appearance, such as text style, the line and fill color, or the author name used for the comment. The most efficient way to do this is by using the Properties Bar.

Choose View > Toolbars > Properties Bar to open the toolbar. You can leave it floating in the program window or drag it to dock with the other toolbars. The content of the Properties Bar changes depending on the object selected on the document page.

Click the comment icon on the document page to select it. In the Properties Bar you see the name on the toolbar change to Note Properties.

Click the color swatch and choose a color for the note box from the color palette.

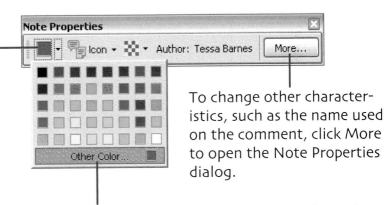

To change other character-istics, such as the name used on the comment, click More to open the Note Properties dialog.

If you want to use a custom color, click Other Color on the color palette to open a Color Picker.

change note appearance

Click Icon to open a pull-down list of options you can select for the comment's icon on the document page.

To specify an opacity level for the comment, click Opacity to open a percentage list and choose an option.

You can also use the Properties Bar to change the appearance of the text in a comment's note box. Click inside the note box, and the Properties Bar displays text options.

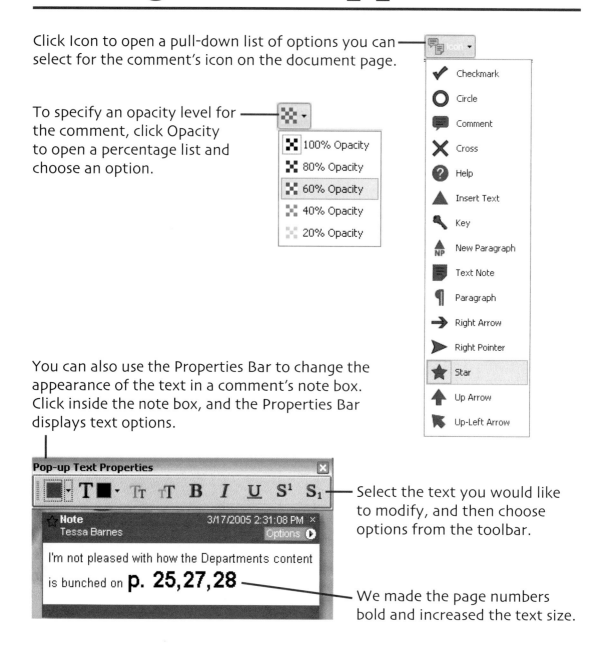

Select the text you would like to modify, and then choose options from the toolbar.

We made the page numbers bold and increased the text size.

edit the text

Acrobat and Adobe Reader include special types of comments called Text Edits that let you indicate places to replace, delete, or insert text. To make the process even simpler, once you start you can just use keyboard commands to add the comments and edits. Follow these steps to select text to be edited:

1 Click the Text Edits tool on the Commenting toolbar to open its submenu.

2 Click the Indicate Text Edits Tool on the submenu.

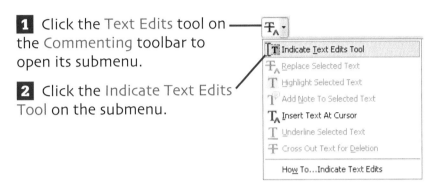

3 Click and drag with the tool to select text. You can increase or decrease the amount of text selected by dragging one of the small arrows at the corners of the highlighted text.

06 Brooke's Musings: A new regular feature on living and working in Asia.

Now that you've selected the text, you can do one of several things with it.

If you want to delete the text:

Select Cross Out Text for Deletion from the Text Edit menu.

06 Brooke's Musings: A ~~new~~ —— Press [Delete] or [Backspace] on the keyboard to delete the text, shown as a cross-out through the selected text.
on living and working in Asia.

edit the text (cont.)

If you want to add an explanation of your edit, double-click the deletion using the Hand tool 🖑 to open a Cross-Out note box where you can type a comment, question, or note.

If you want to replace the text:

Select the piece of text on the page, and choose Replace Selected Text from the Text Edit menu.

09 Tots in Thailand: ~~Exotic beaches and fascinating history isn't just for adults~~ read about one family's adventures.

Replacement Text 3/16/2005 1:22:31 PM

Tessa Barnes Options

Trading in backpacks for diaper bags

A caret is shown at the location the replacement text starts.

Start typing your new suggested text. The existing text is crossed out automatically and your replacement text is shown in a note box.

If you want to insert additional text:

Click the location in a block of text with the Indicate Text Edits Tool where you want to insert some text and start typing. The text you type appears in a note box.

A caret is shown on the page at the insertion point.

attach a file comment

In both Acrobat and Adobe Reader, you can use a file as a comment. Sounds strange doesn't it? But it makes a lot of sense. In the project, our reviewer Tessa doesn't like one of the images on the third page of the project. She can illustrate her point by attaching the image she DOES like, following these steps:

1 Click the Attach a File as a Comment tool 📎 on the Commenting toolbar.

2 Move the pointer over the page—it will change to resemble a pushpin—and click where you want the comment's icon placed. In the resulting Add Attachment dialog, locate and select the file you want to attach, and click Select to dismiss the dialog. In the project, the attached file is named orchidB.tif.

3 The File Attachment Properties dialog opens.

4 Make changes to the appearance of the comment icon as desired. I am using the default Attachment icon (push-pin,) but changed the color to bright yellow for contrast.

5 Click Close to dismiss the File Attachment Properties dialog.

6 A Document Status icon now shows at the lower left of the program window. Move your pointer over the icon and hold it for a couple of seconds to see information about the attachment in a tooltip.

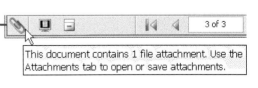

This document contains 1 file attachment. Use the Attachments tab to open or save attachments.

add a stamp comment

Stamps are applied to a page just like old-fashioned ink stamps, but won't get your fingers dirty. You can choose from a smorgasbord of stamps in Acrobat and Adobe Reader. You can also create your own stamps, and store a list of favorites.

In our project, we are going to place a Reviewed stamp on the second page of the project file. The stamp is called a dynamic stamp, meaning that it shows the date and time it's added, as well as the identity of the reviewer.

1 Click the Stamp tool on the Commenting toolbar to open its menu, and then click Dynamic to open the next submenu.

The custom category is my personal collection of stamps; you won't have this listing in your menu unless you've created a custom stamp category.

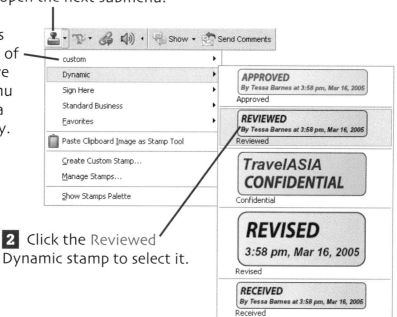

2 Click the Reviewed Dynamic stamp to select it.

3 Move your pointer over the page, and click where you want to place the comment. The stamp will show up with your name, and the current date and time. The stamp is semi-transparent.

4 If you want to resize the stamp, click and drag one of its corner handles.

5 Double-click the stamp on the page to open a note box and type any additional text you want to include.

add a callout

The originator of the project file enables the Drawing Markups toolbar in their Acrobat preferences before sending for review. Some of the options are all-purpose tools, while others are designed more for the scribblers among us. Acrobat 7 and Reader 7 offer the Callout tool, which lets you use callouts, a combination of both a text box and a jointed arrow. This saves having to add two separate comments, such as a text box and an arrow. A callout's content is always visible on the page. That is, its text content isn't in a collapsible note box, as other comment types are.

To add a callout to the project:

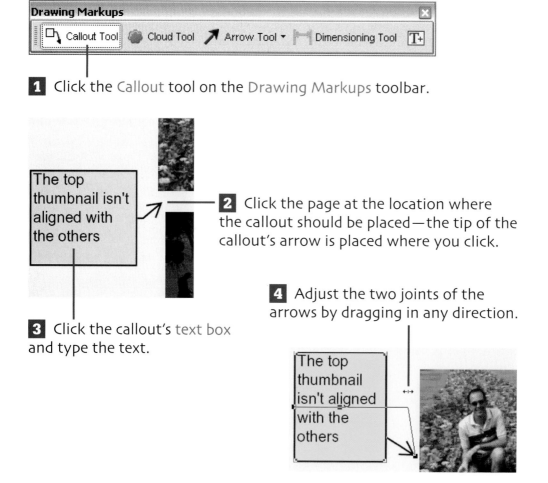

1 Click the Callout tool on the Drawing Markups toolbar.

The top thumbnail isn't aligned with the others

2 Click the page at the location where the callout should be placed—the tip of the callout's arrow is placed where you click.

4 Adjust the two joints of the arrows by dragging in any direction.

3 Click the callout's text box and type the text.

The top thumbnail isn't aligned with the others

apply drawing markups

The last comment we'll add to the file uses one of the Drawing tools. You can use basic shapes and freehand drawings as comments—Acrobat's way of providing doodling and scribbling options to commenters! As with all comments, you can modify a drawing comment's appearance and subject/author labels.

Follow these steps to add a rectangle shape to the file:

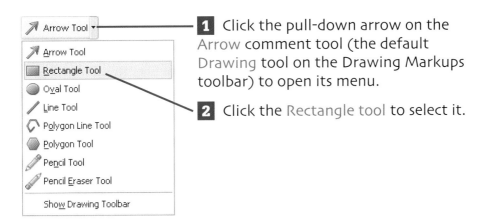

1 Click the pull-down arrow on the Arrow comment tool (the default Drawing tool on the Drawing Markups toolbar) to open its menu.

2 Click the Rectangle tool to select it.

3 Drag a rectangle shape on the page with the tool— you see a hatched line as you drag the mouse. Release the mouse to complete the Rectangle comment.

4 Double-click the rectangle's shape to open a note box.

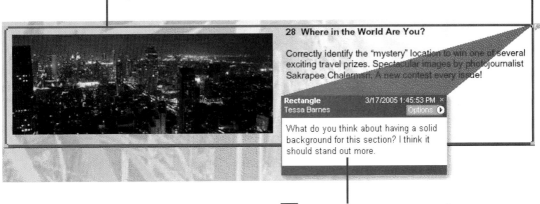

5 Type text as required.

When you click off the comment, the note box is closed, and you see the comment icon at the edge of the rectangle 🔲.

send the comments back

Our final job as a participant in the review is to send the comments back to the originator of the review (who is, of course, ourselves).

1 Click Send Comments 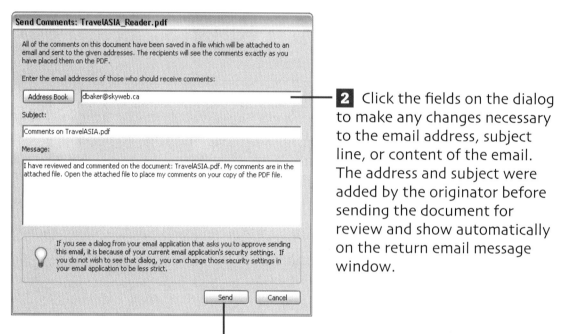 on the Commenting toolbar to open the Send Comments:[name of file] dialog.

2 Click the fields on the dialog to make any changes necessary to the email address, subject line, or content of the email. The address and subject were added by the originator before sending the document for review and show automatically on the return email message window.

3 Click Send. The dialog closes and the file is sent.

Depending on the configuration of your computer, you may see an Outgoing Message Notification dialog—click OK to dismiss the dialog and send your file.

extra bits

change your comment identity p. 38

- Rather than changing the commentor's identity in the Properties dialog, set it in the program preferences instead. Choose Edit > Preferences (Acrobat > Preferences on Mac) and select Identity in the categories column on the left. In the Identity settings enter text such as your name, title, email address, and so. The preferences can be changed in both Adobe Reader and Acrobat.

- Ths is the information that will appear in dynamic stamps and note comments.

use a comment's options menu p. 39

- To change a comment's appearance, you can use its Options menu. Click the Options button on the Note box to display the Options menu.

- Click Properties to open the Properties dialog, showing the Appearance tab. Choose custom options such as the color or icon.

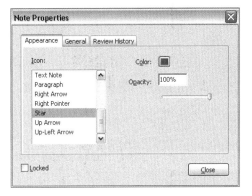

- Select the General tab and change the name of the commenter; you can also change the subject.

extra bits

set a default appearance p. 39

- After setting a custom appearance for any type of comment, you can set it as the new default. Right-click/Ctrl-click the comment's icon to open the shortcut menu, and choose Make Current Properties Default. From now on, each time a comment of the same type is added, it uses the same visual features.

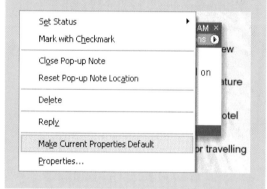

comment appearance strategies p. 39

- Change the appearance of a comment based on your workflow, policies, or procedures. If you are involved in a large review, colors may be assigned to workgroups for ease of identification—for example, red for marketing, blue for designers, and so on.

- You might want to use different icons to represent different topic areas. For example, use the "question mark" icon ❷ when you want to ask a general question, or use the "insert text" icon ▲ if you want to make a comment about missing content.

showing hidden text edit comments p. 41

- To see the content of a comment when it's closed, move your pointer over the edit—you see the text in a tooltip.

add comments

text edits or highlight comments? p. 41

- The Commenting toolbar includes both the Text Edit highlight tool and Highlighting tools, which make up their own subtoolbar on the Commenting toolbar. Although both look much the same on the PDF document, there is a difference. The Text Edit highlight comments can be exported into a source Word document in Windows, while the Highlight comments are simply highlights used to point out features or content in the PDF file.

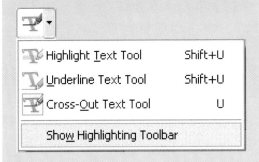

viewing attachments p. 43

- Using an attached file as a comment is a safe way to send extra files along with your other comments: The file is attached to the comment, and won't be lost or misplaced.
- You can open the attached file right from Acrobat or Adobe Reader. Select the Attachments tab to display the pane across the bottom of the program window. Double-click the listing, or click the Open attachment button on the pane's toolbar to open the file.

- To quickly open an attached file, double-click the comment icon on the page to open the file. You may see a Launch Attachment dialog asking about opening the file format—choose an open option and click OK.

extra bits

tracking as a reviewer p. 48

- If you are working in Adobe Reader as a participant, you can check the review's status in Reader's version of the Tracker. Click the pull-down arrow of the Comment & Markup Task button to open its menu and choose Tracker.

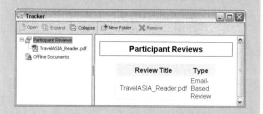

- Reader's Tracker is very similar to the one we used in Acrobat when we were setting up the review. However, as you can only initiate and manage a review from within Acrobat, only participant reviews are listed in Reader's version of the Tracker.

returning comments p. 48

- The document and its comments are returned as a PDF file attached to the email from Adobe Reader. If you are working in Acrobat you can send either the entire document and the comments as a PDF file, or the comments only as an FDF file.

add comments

6. import and sort comments

In this phase of the project, you are going back to the role of the review originator, or initiator again, and we are also returning to Acrobat 7 Professional.

One of your major tasks in managing a review is compiling the comments from all your reviewers into a copy of your master file. So you don't have to keep track of which files are which, and whether or not comments have been added, Acrobat can take care of the details for you when you are using a review, as you'll see. We'll also take a tour of the Comments pane, and look at how comments are displayed.

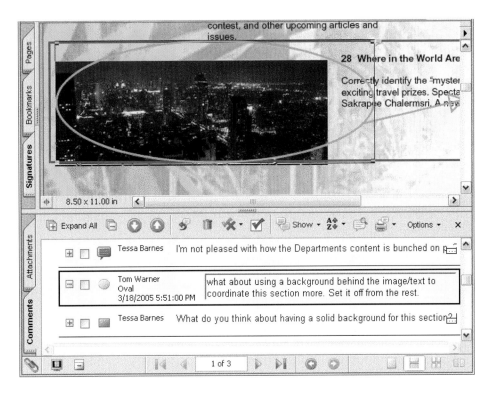

get comments via e-mail

The reviewers (in this case, you) have made comments on the PDF and have sent them back to the originator (you again!) As a reviewer, you didn't have to remember who to email the comments to, as the wizard used to set up the review also included the email address for returning the comments.

The comments return to you attached to emails that tell you you can store the PDF with its comments on your hard drive, or open the file immediately. The next thing to do is to bring the various reviewers' comments into your original PDF file so that you can begin to make the requested changes.

Working as the review initiator/originator, follow these steps to open a reviewed file and incorporate it into a review document:

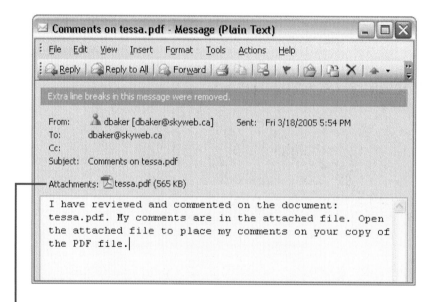

1 In your email program, double-click the attachment to the received email. The file uses the name of the original file, unless the recipient saved the file with a different name before sending it to you (as shown in the example).

2 Acrobat 7 opens automatically, and shows a Merge Comments? dialog, asking if you want to merge the comments into the original document used for the review or to open a copy only.

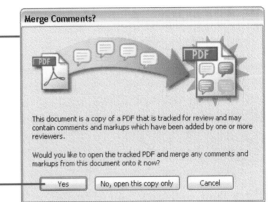

3 Click Yes to dismiss the dialog.

4 The original review document opens showing the Comments pane.

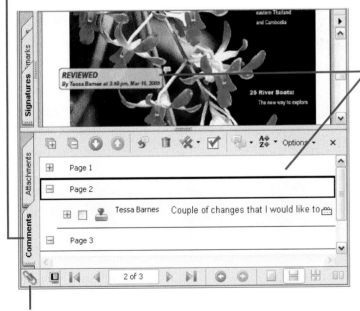

5 The comments are placed on the document and listed in the Comments pane.

6 Choose File > Save or use Ctrl S/⌘ S to save the file. The project sample file is saved as TravelASIA1.pdf.

The imported comments include one created with the Attach a File as a Comment tool—you see the Attachment Document Status icon shown at the bottom of the program window.

import comment files

As the originator of a review, you might receive PDF or comment FDF files by email, and, rather than opening them immediately, you can save them to your hard drive like any other type of email attachment to work with at another time. When you're ready to work with the comments, importing them into the file uses a slightly different process than if you had done so upon receiving them.

Follow these steps to import a comment file from your hard drive:

1 Open the reviewed document in Acrobat 7.

2 Choose the Comments tab to display the Comments pane across the bottom of the program window.

3 Click the Options button on the Comments pane to open its menu and choose Import Comments.

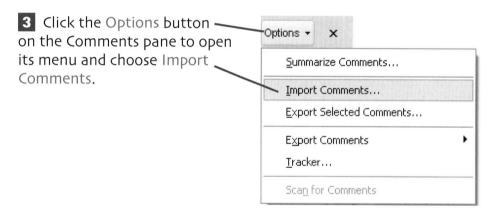

import and sort comments

4 In the Import Comments dialog, locate and choose the FDF or PDF file(s) you saved to your hard drive.

5 Click Select to close the Import Comments dialog.

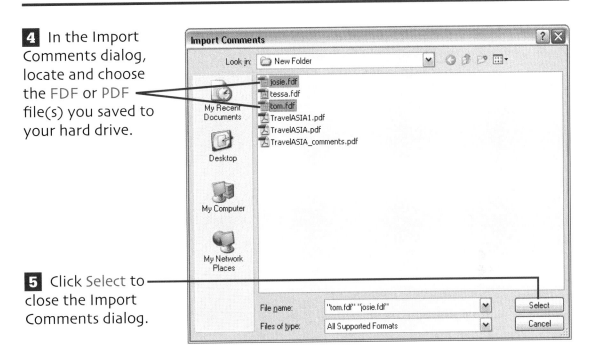

6 If you saved copies of the original reviewing document after adding comments, you may see an dialog asking if you want to import the comments, as it doesn't recognize the file as the same one as your review document.

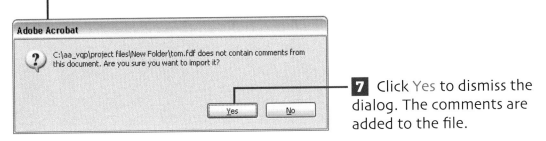

7 Click Yes to dismiss the dialog. The comments are added to the file.

8 Save the file again; it's a good idea to save a copy of your file that is separate from the original master file in case you have to modify the source file at a later time. The sample project file, containing comments from all three reviewers, is saved as TravelASIA2.pdf.

tour the comments pane

The rest of the project centers around the Comments pane. Before we get into details, let's take a look at what's in it:

First the toolbar:

Navigation tools open and close the comments listings and move through the list.

Management tools are used for finding comments in different ways, as well as for printing.

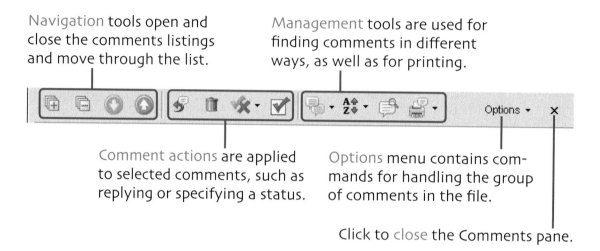

Comment actions are applied to selected comments, such as replying or specifying a status.

Options menu contains commands for handling the group of comments in the file.

Click to close the Comments pane.

In the Comment pane itself:

The Comments list contains information about the comments added in the review.

Comment contains more text than shown in the pane.

This page of com- ments is open; (-) means the page's content is displayed.

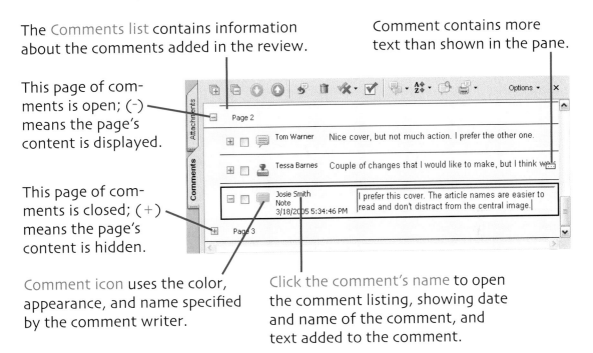

This page of com- ments is closed; (+) means the page's content is hidden.

Comment icon uses the color, appearance, and name specified by the comment writer.

Click the comment's name to open the comment listing, showing date and name of the comment, and text added to the comment.

sort the comments

To help organize your work in the Comments pane, you can sort comments in a number of different ways. Sorting shows all the comments in your document—they are merely arranged using different methods such as page, author, or type of comment. When you import comments in an Acrobat review document, they are already sorted using the default sort by page method.

To choose a different sorting method:

1 Click the Sort By button on the Comments pane to open its pull-down menu; the current sorting method is checked on the menu.

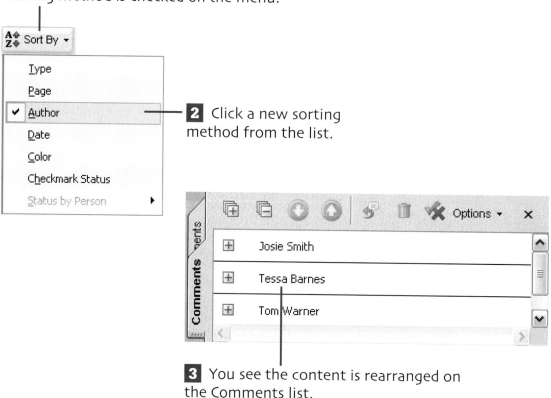

2 Click a new sorting method from the list.

3 You see the content is rearranged on the Comments list.

filter the comments

In our project, we have only a couple dozen comments, but reviews conducted in a workgroup can have hundreds of comments. It's hard to decide where to start in a case like that, but I'll show you a way you can make your work simpler.

A filter is not the same as a sort order, even though you have similar choices in the menu. When a filter is applied, only those comments fitting the options you chose are shown in the Comments pane; all others are hidden.

To apply a filter, follow these steps:

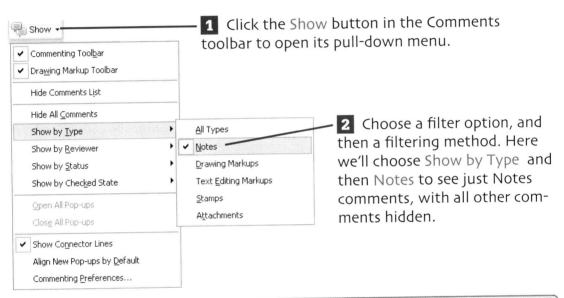

1 Click the Show button in the Comments toolbar to open its pull-down menu.

2 Choose a filter option, and then a filtering method. Here we'll choose Show by Type and then Notes to see just Notes comments, with all other comments hidden.

3 An information dialog opens explaining that replies are hidden; click OK to dismiss the dialog and filter the Comments list.

Click Don't show again to hide the information dialog in the future.

filter the comments (cont.)

4 On the Comments pane, a yellow status message indicates that some of the comments are hidden because of the applied filter.

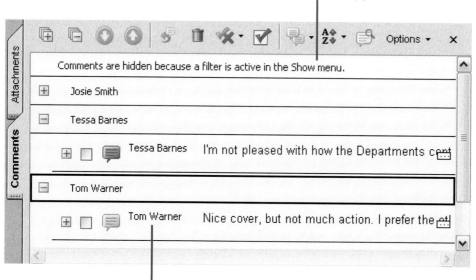

5 Only the specified type of comment is shown for each author. The list was sorted by author; when the list is filtered, the results are shown according to the selected sorting method.

import and sort comments

extra bits

controlling the review process p. 56

- If you're the person starting a review, all comments are returned to you. To maintain control of the review process, you, as the initiator, should control invitations to the review.

- If you as the initiator invite reviewers, the participants are listed in your Tracker window, which isn't the case if someone else invites participants.

- If you initiate the reviews the comments automatically return to you and can be incorporated into the original document; if others invite participants, who knows where those comment files might end up.

comment files p. 56

- There are three comment files available for download from the book's Web site, named tessa.fdf, tom.fdf, and josie.fdf. The tessa.fdf file is the set of comments created in the previous chapter.

importing files p. 56

- Following this project as both originator and participant using the same file can be confusing if you are working on the same computer. If you find it difficult to bring your own comments back into the original file that you specified for the review, use the comment files available from the book's Web site.

removing a filter p. 61

- Fortunately, Acrobat reminds you whenever there is an active filter on comments. To remove the filter, choose the reverse of the commands you originally selected for the filter. For example, if you chose Show > Show by Type > Notes to filter the comments and show only the Notes, choose Show > Show by Type > All Types to remove the filter.

extra bits

managing the review p. 54

- In a perfect world, starting a review would be a one-shot deal: You send the invitations, and your reviewers busily review the document and return comments to you promptly. However, Acrobat handles real-life, not-so-perfect situations by letting you add more people to an existing review if you have forgotten to invite someone, and allowing you to send reminder emails to your participants who are late in sending comments back to you.

- Click the Send for Review Task button and choose Tracker to open the Tracker window. Click the review you want to work with in the My Reviews listing at the left of the dialog to select it.

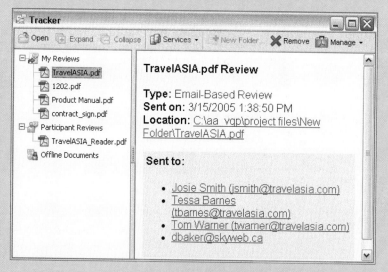

- Click Manage to open a set of options that allow you to send reminders and emails and invite others to participate in the review.

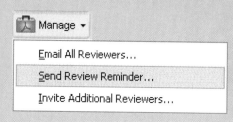

7. working with review returns

Once we import reviewers' feedback, we have a number of comments in our review document—now what? What happens next depends on the workflow you are using. Fortunately, Acrobat's tools and features will accomodate whatever you intend to do with the comments.

If you are responsible for carrying out modifications to the review file based on the recommendations of the reviewers, you can use check marks to indicate which ones you have dealt with. If you need to locate a specific comment, Acrobat lets you search the content of comments in your document.

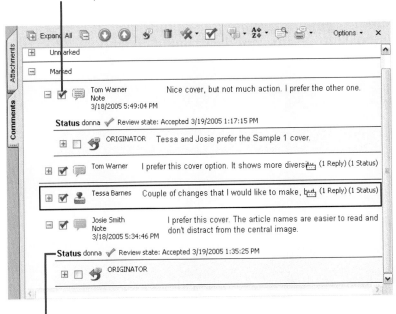

If you are responsible for compiling reviewers' comments, and then recirculating the file for a second round of reviewing or to store the comments and the document in report form, you will find the Review Status options useful.

search comments

If you have a long document and/or a document containing a great number of comments, it can be difficult finding a particular one. You can pinpoint specific comments using Acrobat's Search PDF window. In our project, we are going to find the comments that refer to the magazine covers, as one of the tasks in the project is to decide which cover to use.

1 Click Search comments 🖳 on the Comment pane's tools to open the Search PDF window at the right side of the program window.

2 Type the word or phrase to use as the search term in the Search PDF window. To find the comments about the cover, I typed cover as the search term.

3 Choose other search options.

4 Click Search Comments.

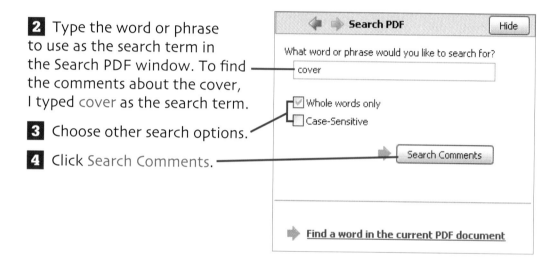

5 Acrobat processes the file and displays the results.

6 In our project, there are four comments that include the search term, listed in the Results area— two of the results refer to the same comment.

7 Move the mouse over the listing; you see the page number containing the listed comment shown in a tooltip.

8 Click the result in the Search PDF Results list.

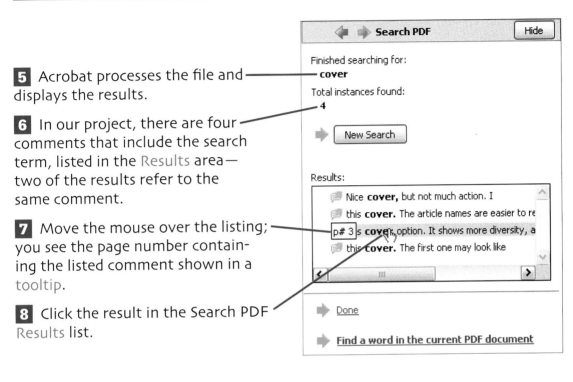

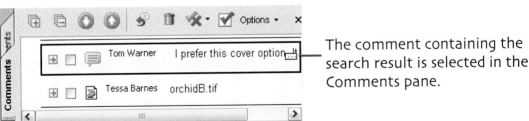

The comment containing the search result is selected in the Comments pane.

Leave the Search PDF window open for now—next you'll see what you can do with search results.

check-mark comments

Acrobat provides check marks as a way to keep track of comments as you're going through them. You can use check marks for anything you like—to indicate comments you need to confirm with a colleague, those that you'd like to export to a text file or a spreadsheet, or comments you want to come back to before your work session is finished. In fact, any time you need to mark comments for reference, you can use check marks. The check mark system you use in Acrobat is internal, which means the check marks are shown in your copy of the file, but aren't sent to anyone else if you recirculate comments to reviewers.

In our project, we are going to use check marks to identify comments the participants made about their preferred magazine cover.

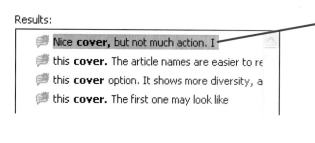

1 In the Results listing on the Search PDF window, click the first search result. The comment is selected on the Comments pane.

2 Click the Checkmark button ☑ on the Comments pane.

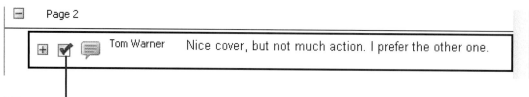

3 The check box to the left of the comment's information shows a blue check mark.

4 Select the second instance of the word in the Results list.

5 A Search dialog displays, and asks if you want to repeat the search since the file is modified when you add the check mark. Click Do not show this message again.

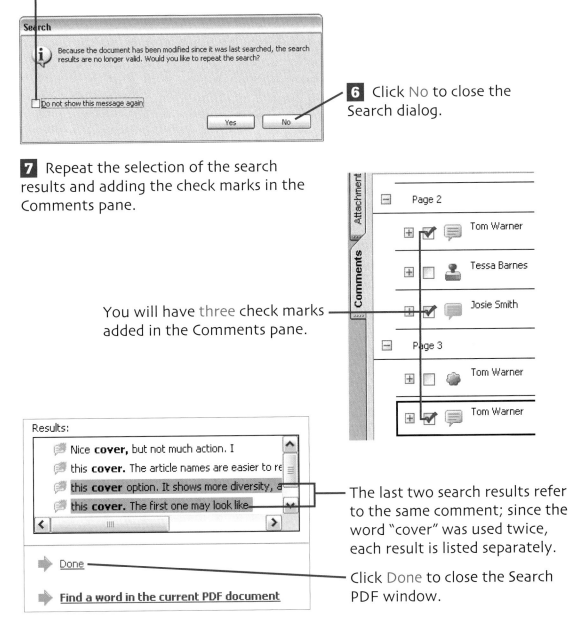

6 Click No to close the Search dialog.

7 Repeat the selection of the search results and adding the check marks in the Comments pane.

You will have three check marks added in the Comments pane.

The last two search results refer to the same comment; since the word "cover" was used twice, each result is listed separately.

Click Done to close the Search PDF window.

add check marks

There are three check marks in the Comments list now, and there are three reviewers in the project. But there is no check mark identifying the opinion of our first reviewer, Tessa Barnes, as she didn't use the word cover in her comments. We'll find and mark the comment that includes her feedback about the magazine covers.

1 In the Comments pane, click the Sort By button ↕ Sort By ▾ and choose Author from its pull-down menu. You see the comments are now sorted according to the names of the participants.

2 Click the Tessa Barnes listing in the Comments pane to open the list of her comments.

3 Scroll down the list to the Stamp from Tessa. The text added to the comment specifies that she liked the first sample cover best.

4 Click the check box to the left of the Stamp icon in the comment's row to add a check mark. You could also click the Checkmark button on the Comments pane's tools.

			Tessa Barnes	
⊞	☐	🗅	Tessa Barnes	The top thumbnail isn't aligned with the others
⊞	☐	T̯ₐ	Tessa Barnes	Trading in backpacks for diaper bags
⊞	☐	T̲	Tessa Barnes	Brooke's column was a new feature a few months
⊟	☐	Tₐ	Tessa Barnes	written by our own Canadian expat on
⊟	☑	🏷	Tessa Barnes Reviewed 3/19/2005 11:24:21 AM	Couple of changes that I would like to make, but I think we are coming along nicely! I like sample 1 best.
⊞	☐	💬	Tessa Barnes	I'm not pleased with how the Departments content

We've check-marked cover opinions from each of the reviewers. Now click the Sort By button on the Comments pane again and choose Checkmark Status. Acrobat sorts the comments into two groups—those with check marks, and those without.

Click the Marked heading to open the listing. You see four comments with checkmarks.

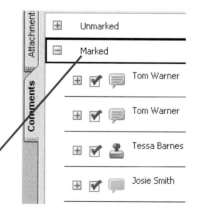

reply to comments

You can reply to comments, either as the review initiator or as a participant. If we were doing a second round of reviewing, our participants could read and respond to our replies; in this case, the replies are added to the file and are seen in the summary report (described in the next chapter). The comments that we'll reply to are the check marked ones that indicate the reviewers' preferred magazine cover sample.

1 Click to select the first checked comment on the Comments list.

2 Click Reply on the Comments pane's tools.

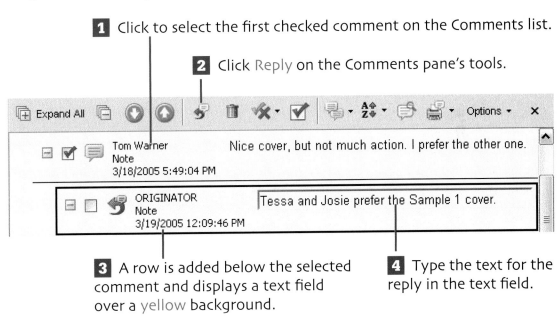

3 A row is added below the selected comment and displays a text field over a yellow background.

4 Type the text for the reply in the text field.

reply to comments

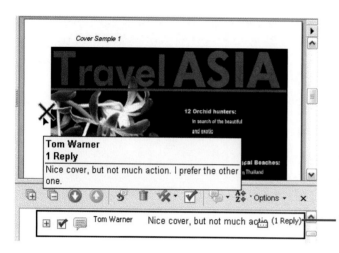

When the comment is collapsed in the Comments pane, a notation shows on the comment's row.

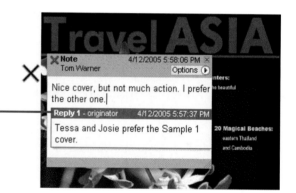

Check the document page—you see the reply overlays the Note for the original comment.

5 Add replies to the other checked comments.

set a comment's status

When you want to communicate to your reviewers about a collection of comments, or to help you keep track of how you've dealt with them, you can choose a Review status or state for the comments. Like check marks, a review state can be used to identify how a comment has been processed. In our project, the comments that have a check mark (and a reply) will be assigned a Review state of Accepted.

1 Select the first comment with a check mark.

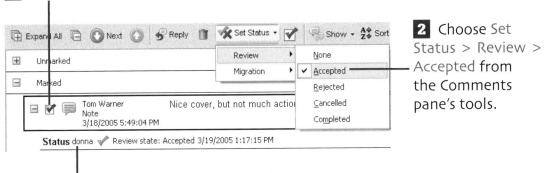

2 Choose Set Status > Review > Accepted from the Comments pane's tools.

3 The Review state is shown below the comment details, and includes the status and the time/date.

4 Select the next comment with a check mark, and again assign a Review state. Continue with the remaining checked comments in the project.

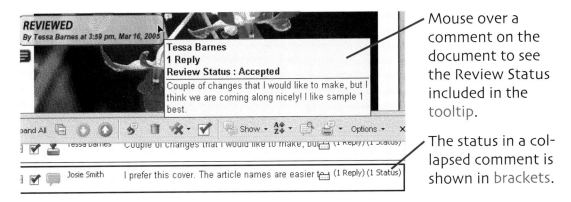

Mouse over a comment on the document to see the Review Status included in the tooltip.

The status in a collapsed comment is shown in brackets.

extra bits

specifying search terms p. 66

- You can search for terms very precisely in Acrobat, which can be both good and bad. In our project, we searched for the term "cover." If we had used the term "Cover"—with a capital "C"—and chosen the Case-Sensitive search option, we'd have had no results for the search.

more on using check marks p. 68

- Decide how you want to use check marks in your workflow. Our project used one example; you can use them any time you need to keep track of a number of comments.

- You may see a dialog explaining that check marks are only for internal file use. Once you have read it, click Do not show this message again to save a mouse click for each check mark you add.

modifying comment replies p. 71

- You can change the characteristics of a reply you add to a comment just as you change the characteristics of any other type of comment, as Acrobat defines a reply as a modified Note. Choose View > Toolbars > Properties Bar to display the Properties bar.

- Using the Properties bar, you can change the characteristics of the reply such as the color or text— you might use italics or a certain color to identify responses more clearly on the document page, for example.

- To change other details, such as the name and subject, right-click/Ctrl-click the comment to open the shortcut menu and choose Properties to open the Note Properties dialog. Change the name or subject on the General tab.

following along in the file p. 71

- If you'd like to see this book's project file including all the reviewers' comments as well as the originator's replies and the review status, download the TravelASIA3.pdf file from the book's Web site.

what "status" means p. 73

- The available Review Status options include None (the default), Accepted, Rejected, Cancelled, or Completed.

- In a large or complex review, specify beforehand how the status will be defined, by whom, and what it represents. That way, if you are working with hundreds of comments from many reviewers, your review participants will know exactly what you mean by a status. For example, if you have made a change in the document as a result of the comment you might specify the comment as "Completed." In other reviews, "Completed" may mean that a comment has been added in the first round of a review.

filtering and sorting by status p. 73

- Setting a status can be a good way of handling lots of comments in a project. Choose Show > Show by Status > Review and select a state option from the Comment pane's tools to filter your comments easily and show only those that you have completed, for example.

- A neat way to sort your comments in a big review is by the person who assigned a state to a comment. You need comments with an assigned review status, of course. Then, choose Sort By > Status by Person > and select a name. This way you can see which comments Pat rejected and which ones Terry accepted.

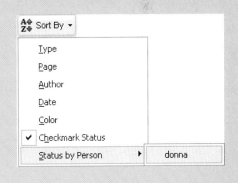

extra bits

selecting comments p. 73

- You can select comments and replies in the Comments pane just as you would other objects on your desktop or in other programs.

- Select comments that you would like to export to a text file or an FDF file for storage outside your review document.

- Click to select a comment, and then [Shift]-click to select the last comment in a contiguous sequence.

- Press [Ctrl]/⌘ and click to select multiple non-contiguous comments.

- If you have closed the sort groups, click a group to select all its contents automatically.

- Selecting comments also selects any replies that have been added to the comments. In the case of setting a status, for example, you will have one Review state assigned for each of the comment and the reply.

working with review returns

8. finishing a review

Our file contains comments from the reviewers on the artwork, text, and cover sample preferences for our magazine project. The way we conduct the rest of the review depends on our workflow, how independent the members of our team are, and the intent and purpose of the review.

For instance, we may want to make the revisions to the file and then recirculate it for a second round of review and approval from our participants. On the other hand, our participants may be fine with passing along their comments and depending on us to make the necessary revisions independently.

In this chapter, we'll work with the comments, sorting and sending a group of comments to a designer for action. We will create a summary of the comments in the document that can be stored for future reference. We won't send a second round of comments to our participants, but they can view copies of the summary reports if they like.

organize comments

We are going to look at the comments list and identify those for exporting to the magazine's layout designer for repairing image issues.

We'll continue working in the Comments pane to arrange our revisions. First, we'll remove the checkmarks that were used in the last chapter for organizing information about the preferred cover. We'll add other checkmarks in a bit, but they're for organizing different information.

1 Choose Sort By > Checkmark Status to arrange the comments in the project into Unmarked and Marked categories.

2 Click Collapse All to close the comment lists.

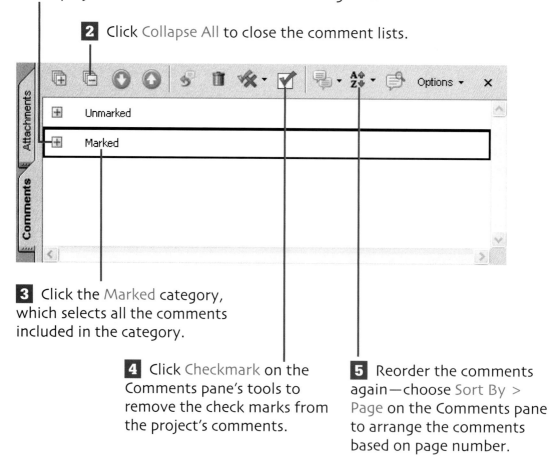

3 Click the Marked category, which selects all the comments included in the category.

4 Click Checkmark on the Comments pane's tools to remove the check marks from the project's comments.

5 Reorder the comments again—choose Sort By > Page on the Comments pane to arrange the comments based on page number.

group comments

Before we get started sorting comments again, let's look at a way to simplify the comments list. Our reviewer, Tom, used a circle and an arrow to make his point about using a background at the bottom of page 1. In Acrobat 7 you can group the comments rather than dealing with two comments for the same thing. Follow these steps to group the comments:

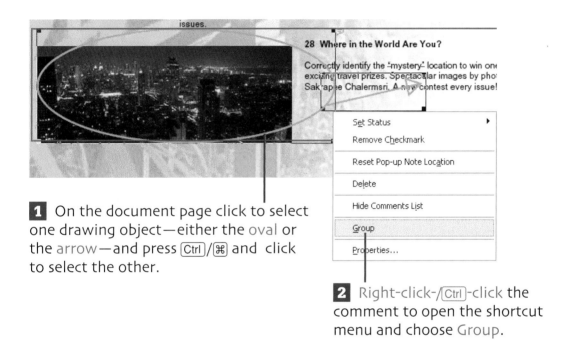

1 On the document page click to select one drawing object—either the oval or the arrow—and press Ctrl/⌘ and click to select the other.

2 Right-click-/Ctrl-click the comment to open the shortcut menu and choose Group.

3 The objects are combined into one unit—in the Comments pane you see the icon is replaced by a neat little image of grouped objects.

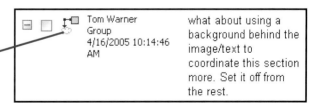

select comments

Now we can get down to business and see what needs addressing by our graphic designer. Let's add check marks to those comments we want to send to the graphic designer for correction in the source file.

First be sure to size the program window at a convenient size so you can see the Document pane clearly and also read the contents in the Comments list.

1 Click (+) to the left of Page 1 to open the list of comments; the indicator changes to (-).

2 Read through the comments. Tessa says the top thumbnail image isn't aligned; that's a job for our graphic designer.

3 Click the check box to the left of the comment's icon to add a check mark.

4 Two reviewers commented that they'd like to see a background behind the text and image at the bottom of the page; add check marks to both these comments.

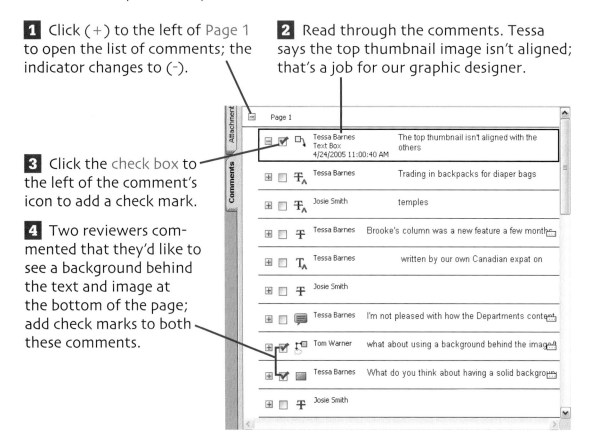

export comments

It isn't necessary for everyone involved in a project to deal with every comment—it's helpful to filter out the pertinent comments and export only those. The comments we have checked are going to be sorted and then exported to our graphic designer for action.

1 Click Sort By to open the pull-down menu and choose Checkmark Status.

2 Choose Show > Show by Checked Status > Checked. On the Comments pane, a warning about the applied filter displays, and only the comments we checked are listed.

3 Click (+) to the left of Marked to open the list of comments; the indicator changes to (-).There are three checked comments we'll export for the designer.

4 Make sure the label Marked is still selected in the Comments pane; if not, click the label to select it.

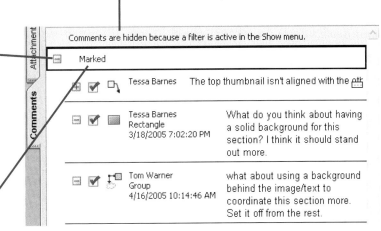

export comments (cont.)

5 Click the Options button on the Comments pane's tools and select Export Selected Comments.

6 A Save As dialog opens; store the file in the same folder as your originals. The comments will be exported as FDFs.

track your progress

Make sure to keep track of what you are doing with comments as you go along. It's a simple task in our project, but that's certainly not always the case. We have sent the comments we need the designer to address. While they are still identified by checkmarks, we can easily attach a Review status to the comments to indicate we have taken action.

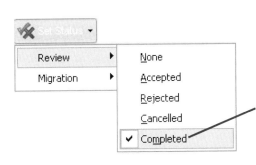

1 The Marked comments are still the only ones showing in the Comments pane. Click the Marked label to select the set of checked comments.

2 Choose Set Status > Review > Completed from the Comments pane's toolbar.

3 A notation is made on all comments at once stating the status and details.

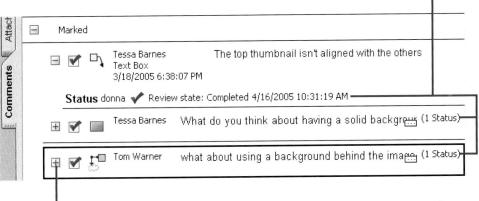

You can see the status notation whether the comment is opened or collapsed.

4 We used the check marks as a way of sorting the comments to send to the designer; now that that's finished, we can remove them. Click the Marked heading again to select all the checked comments and click the Checkmark on the Comments pane's tools to remove the set of checkmarks.

5 Display all the comments again by choosing Show > Show by Checked Status > Checked and Unchecked.

finishing a review   **83**

summarize comments

The last task we are going to do is to create a summary of the comments in the project. Summaries are used to show both the content in the document and the comments and actions taken by the participants, and are useful for maintaining a record of a review cycle. In the Comments pane, click the Options button, and choose Summarize Comments; to open the Summarize Options dialog.

Choose the page layout. I have chosen Document and comments with connector lines on single pages, and used the default paper and font sizes.

Select a paper size.

How do you want the comments sorted?

Do you want to see all the comments, or only the ones showing in the program window?

Choose a font size.

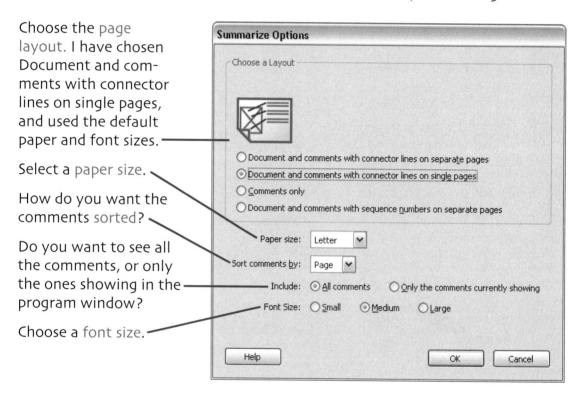

So what does the summary show?

A callout leads to information about the comment on the right side of the page.

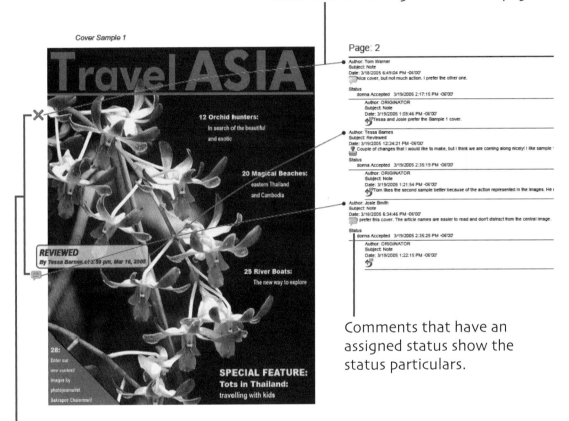

Comments that have an assigned status show the status particulars.

Each comment in the document is shown on the left side of the page.

Choose File > Save to save the file for future reference, just as you save any other type of PDF file. I saved the summary report from the project as Summary of Comments on TravelASIA.pdf.

remove the review

The very last piece of business to take care of is to remove the review from the Tracker. Removing the document from the Tracker's listings doesn't affect the file itself, merely the tracking process Acrobat otherwise maintains.

1 Click the Send for Review Task button ![Send for Review] to open its menu and choose Tracker.

2 In the Tracker window, select the TravelASIA.pdf review file in the My Reviews listing.

3 Click Remove on the Tracker's tools.

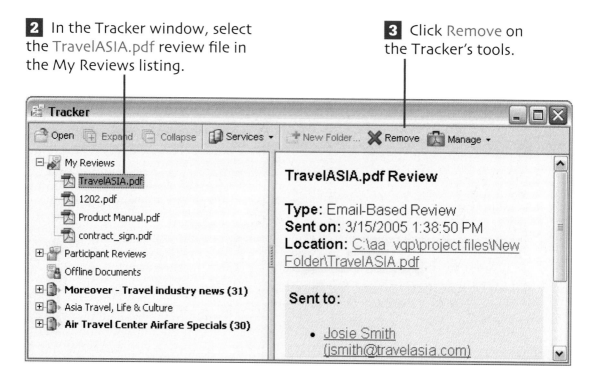

4 Click OK on the confirmation dialog that displays.

extra bits

selecting comments for grouping p. 79

- Although the comments can be selected on either the document page or in the Comments list, the Group command is only available from the document page's shortcut menu.

other types of exports p. 80

- In addition to using comments in Acrobat, as we have done in the project, comments can be exported in different formats to integrate into other applications.

- Export the selected files to Auto-CAD for integration into a source drawing.

- Export selected comments into Word for making edits and adding comments to the original source document. The book's Web site includes a bonus file that shows you how comments are used for making edits in a source Word file.

quick prints p. 84

- If you want a quick copy of your file's content and comments and don't need any custom settings, use the Print Comments command in the Comments pane.

- Click the Print Comments button on the Comments pane to open a menu. Choose Print Comments Summary to generate a summary document sent to your printer. When your Print dialog opens choose characteristics for the print job and click Print to print a copy.

- You can also choose Create PDF of Comments Summary to build a summary document using the program defaults. The PDF summary opens in Acrobat, just like the summary document we prepared in the project.

extra bits

types of summaries p. 84

- Choose a type of comment summary that is best for the characteristics of your document and how you intend to use the summary report.

- Use the Document and comments with connector lines on separate pages option if you want to use the summary report onscreen. You can set the two pages side-by-side in Acrobat and see the content clearly.

- Use the Document and comments with connector lines on single pages option if you plan to both read it online and in print. Our project uses this option.

- Use the Comments only option to print a list of the comment details without showing any page content. This option is best for text-heavy documents like big reports or manuals where you have a lot of comments and wanted a printed list of comments to compare against revisions.

- Use the Document and comments with sequence numbers on separate pages option if you have a text-heavy document and intend to print it. The comments are numbered on the document page, and each page of the document is followed by a page of comments with matching numbers.

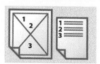

finishing a review

9. editing the pdf file

Our project contains comments from the reviewers on the artwork, text, and cover sample opinions for our project. Depending on your workflow, you can make edits in the PDF file or work with the source files in their native programs. In this chapter, you'll make comments right in the Acrobat PDF file; in the next chapter, you see how comments can be organized and sent to the magazine's graphic designer for action.

If you are working with Acrobat 7 Professional, you can use the TouchUp tools to make changes to text and objects such as images and graphics right in the PDF file, provided the file isn't enabled for commenting in Adobe Reader 7.

In the project, we will edit some text in the Table of Contents page and change one of the images. We will also create a report on the changes to keep for our records.

resave the file

We'll start by saving a copy of the file before making edits. In Chapter 3, you enabled Commenting tools for Adobe Reader 7 users and then circulated that version of the file for the review.

Now, since we want to change content, we have to remove the enabling rights from the file. A file can either be enabled for commenting in Adobe Reader, or it can maintain all its editing capabilities, but not both.

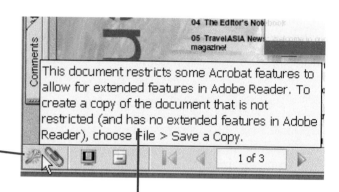

1 Check the file to see if it is enabled. You'll see a document status icon at the lower left of the program window.

If you hold your pointer over the icon, you see information about the enabled file in a tooltip.

2 Choose File > Save a Copy. The Save a Copy information dialog opens and explains that the file you are saving won't have enabling rights. Which, of course, is why you are saving it!

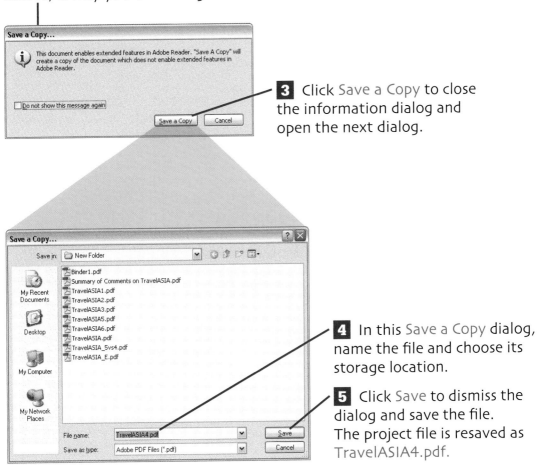

3 Click Save a Copy to close the information dialog and open the next dialog.

4 In this Save a Copy dialog, name the file and choose its storage location.

5 Click Save to dismiss the dialog and save the file. The project file is resaved as TravelASIA4.pdf.

6 Check the lower left of the program window—you won't see the enabled file icon now, and you are ready for editing.

editing the pdf file

organize revisions

There are a few text edits to be made to the first page of the project file, which is the Table of Contents. We are going to make the text and graphic revisions in Acrobat 7 Professional using the TouchUp tools.

In the last chapter, you used check marks to identify the comments explaining the reviewers' choices for the cover. Now we'll remove those check marks and arrange the comments so we can easily identify the revisions to be made in Acrobat.

1 Choose Sort By > Checkmark Status to arrange the comments in the project into Unmarked and Marked categories.

2 Click Collapse All to close the comment lists.

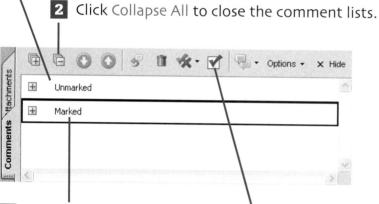

3 Click the Marked category, which selects all the comments included in the category.

4 Click Checkmark on the Comments pane's tools to remove the check marks from the set of comments.

5 Choose Sort By > Page on the Comments pane to arrange the comments based on page number. In the project all of the text and graphic edits we'll make are on the first page.

list comments

Now that the Comments list is sorted by page, we can get down to business. It's simplest to go through the document's comments first and make a list of what needs fixing.

Let's add check marks to those changes we can make in the PDF.

1 First be sure to size the program window at a convenient size so you can both see the Document pane clearly, and read the contents in the Comments list.

2 Click (+) to the left of Page 1 to open the list of comments; the indicator changes to (-).

3 Click the first comment on Page 1 in the Comments pane's list to show its content. Tessa says the top thumbnail image isn't aligned; we can correct that with the TouchUp Object tool.

4 Click the check box to the left of the comment's icon to add a check mark.

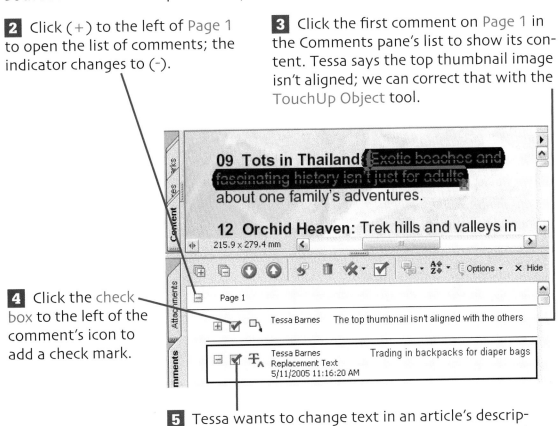

5 Tessa wants to change text in an article's description in the second edit; we can do that easily. Click the check box to add a check mark.

list comments (cont.)

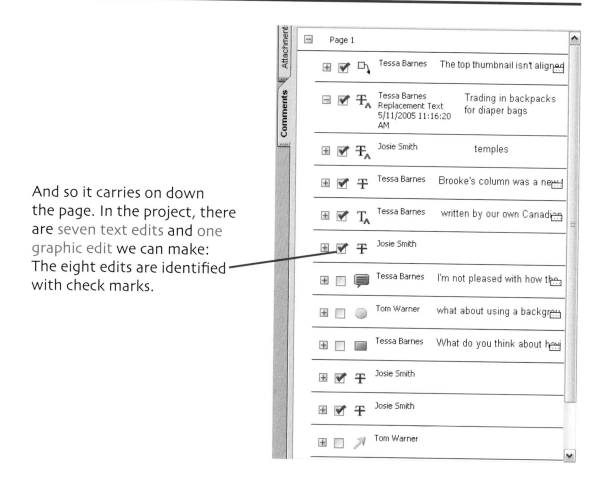

And so it carries on down the page. In the project, there are seven text edits and one graphic edit we can make: The eight edits are identified with check marks.

arrange the window

To make the editing job simpler, arrange the toolbars you need on the program window. Organizing the toolbars when doing a large number of similar tasks can save time and is more convenient.

1 Choose View > Toolbars > Advanced Editing to open the toolbar.

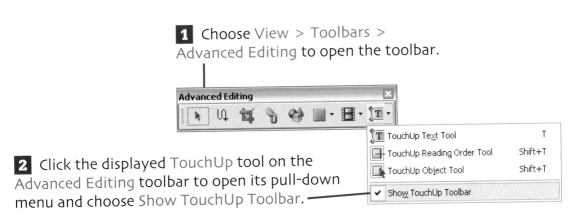

2 Click the displayed TouchUp tool on the Advanced Editing toolbar to open its pull-down menu and choose Show TouchUp Toolbar.

The TouchUp Toolbar opens as a separate toolbar

You see how the toolbars can be arranged for editing sessions like this. I placed the Advanced Editing toolbar up out of the way as none of its other tools are needed for this job.

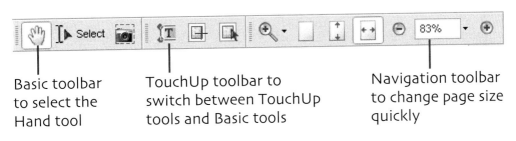

Basic toolbar to select the Hand tool

TouchUp toolbar to switch between TouchUp tools and Basic tools

Navigation toolbar to change page size quickly

editing the pdf file

make text touchups

Now that the program's interface is organized, it's time to make the changes.

The first text edit is in the description of the first article in the Table of Contents.

Before you make the edits, take a second and move the yellow callout out of your way. When you make the text edit in the following steps, some of the text will be hidden below the callout.

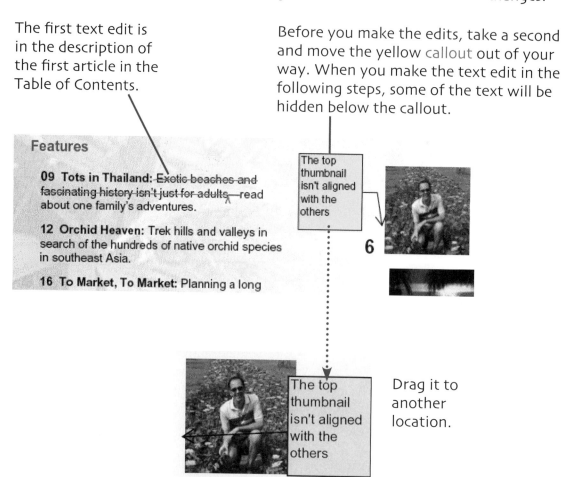

Features

09 Tots in Thailand: Exotic beaches and fascinating history isn't just for adults—read about one family's adventures.

12 Orchid Heaven: Trek hills and valleys in search of the hundreds of native orchid species in southeast Asia.

16 To Market, To Market: Planning a long

The top thumbnail isn't aligned with the others

6

The top thumbnail isn't aligned with the others

Drag it to another location.

editing the pdf file

Tessa Barnes	Trading in backpacks for diaper bags
Replacement Text	
3/18/2005 5:39:24 PM	

1 In the Comments pane triple-click to select the replacement text Tessa wants in the article's description. Press Ctrl/⌘+C to copy the text to the clipboard.

2 Click the TouchUp Text tool [T] on the TouchUp toolbar to select it. Then click and drag to select the text for replacement in the document; the text is shown with a grey highlight.

09 Tots in Thailand: ~~Exotic beaches and fascinating history isn't just for adults~~—read about one family's adventures.

3 Press Ctrl/⌘+V to replace the selected text with the text you copied from the comment.

09 Tots in Thailand: ~~Trading in backpacks~~ for diaper bags ~~—read~~ about one family's adventures.

You'll still see the comment's crossout on the page, as we haven't deleted any of the comments from the document.

You can see that the replacement text lays out differently on the page than the original, primarily because it is shorter. Not to worry—we can fix that easily using the TouchUp Text tool.

09 Tots in Thailand: ~~Trading in backpacks~~
~~for diaper bags~~
——read
about one family's adventures.

4 Click the replacement text after the
word backpacks to place the cursor at that
location and press (Enter)/(Return). The inserted
text is wrapped to the next line.

09 Tots in Thailand: ~~Trading in backpacks~~
~~for diaper bags~~—read
about one family's adventures.

5 Click the text after the word bags, and
press (Delete) to move the rest of the text up
to close the gap in the line.

09 Tots in Thailand: ~~Trading in backpacks~~
~~for diaper bags—read about one family's~~
adventures.

6 Select the phrase about one family's and press
(Ctrl)/(⌘)+(X) to delete it. Click after the word read,
and press (Ctrl)/(⌘)+(V) to paste the text, leaving the
final word adventures alone on the third line.

7 Press (Delete) on the keyboard to remove the
extra space before the final word adventures
on the third line.

track your progress

Make sure to keep track of what you are doing as you go along. We are going to use a Review status option as we work through the edits.

1 Click the comment of Tessa's that we have just worked with in the Comments pane.

2 Choose Set Status > Review > Completed from the Comments pane's toolbar.

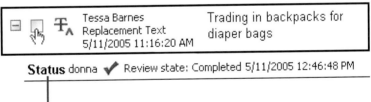

3 A notation is made on the comment stating its status and details

track your progress (cont.)

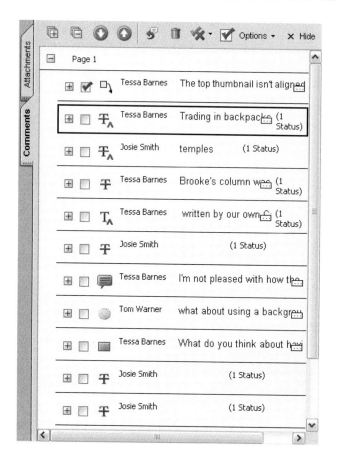

4 Click the check box to remove the check mark—that's one edit finished!

5 Continue with the other text edits in the page, using the TouchUp Text tool.

6 As each edit is complete, set the comment's review status as Complete.

7 Then click the check box to uncheck the comment. Continue until you have completed all the text edits.

editing the pdf file

image touchup

The last check-marked edit in our Comments list is the thumbnail image at the top of the document page. The image is out of alignment, and we are going to use some placement aids to move it precisely.

1 Choose View > Rulers to display horizontal and vertical rulers around the Document pane.

2 Choose View > Guides; we are going to position a guide to help in correctly placing the image.

3 With the Hand tool, move the pointer to the extreme left of the Document pane over the ruler, and then drag right to pull a guide line from the ruler.

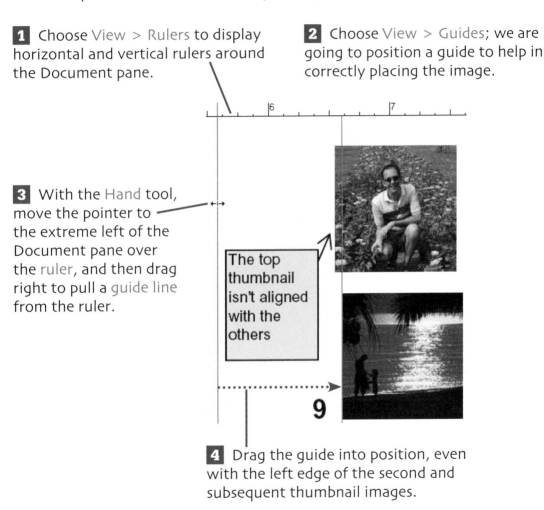

The top thumbnail isn't aligned with the others

4 Drag the guide into position, even with the left edge of the second and subsequent thumbnail images.

image touchup (cont.)

5 Click the TouchUp Object tool ⬚ on the TouchUp toolbar to select it and then click the thumbnail image on the page. You see the image is surrounded by a gray highlight.

6 Drag the image or nudge it by pressing the ➡ key on the keyboard to move the image in line with the other images and the guideline.

7 Record your edit in the Comments pane. Click the comment to select it, and then choose Set Status > Review > Completed from the Comments pane's toolbar.

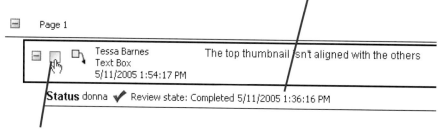

8 Click the check mark to remove it from the check box.

9 Remove the guides and rulers again by choosing View > Guides and View > Rulers.

10 As you have made a lot of changes, choose File > Save As and type a new name. The project's file is named TravelASIA5.pdf.

compare versions

It would be useful to have some way of recording what we have done in the file, in case we need to refer to it in the future. Acrobat offers a way to compare document versions, and you can save a comparison report as a separate PDF file.

In our project, we compare the TravelASIA4.pdf file (complete with all the reviewers' comments) to the TravelASIA5.pdf file (the file after making text and image edits).

Choose Document > Compare Documents to open the Compare Documents dialog.

Specify the documents to compare by clicking the Choose buttons and selecting a file for the Compare and To Document fields. Select our two files.

In the Type Of Comparison section select Textual differences, which will show text that has been inserted, deleted, or moved.

Select the Consolidated Report radio button, which adds markups in the report where the differences occur on the current document.

Compare Documents

Compare (older document)

Document: TravelASIA4.pdf   Choose...

Revision:

To (newer document)

Document: TravelASIA5.pdf   Choose...

Revision:

Type of Comparison

◯ Page by page visual differences   Normal analysis   Markup color: ▢

◉ Textual differences   ☐ Include font information (style, size, typeface)

Choose compare report type

◯ Side by Side Report

◉ Consolidated Report

Help   OK   Cancel

Click OK to close the dialog and run the report.

compare versions (cont.)

Now the review is finished; let's have a look at the results.

The comment on the upper left of the page shows the details of the comparison, listing the documents compared and the number of changes.

Move your pointer over a comment icon on the page to see the changes in a tooltip.

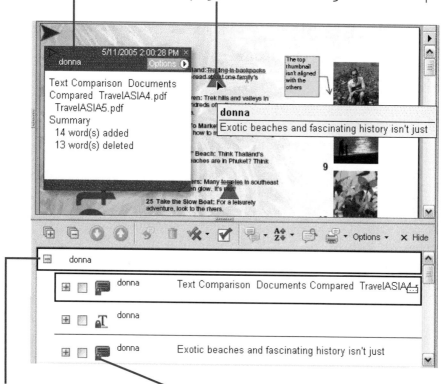

Sort the comments by author; the report results will show your comments using your name.

Comments listed in the Comments pane use different types of comment tools, but all comments are locked— you can't make changes.

Save the file showing report results with a unique name. My file is saved as TravelASIA_5vs4.pdf (that's version 5 vs. version 4.)

editing the pdf file

extra bits

source files p. 92

- The content in this chapter is shown in four files available from the book's Web site.
- TravelASIA_E.pdf is the project complete with comments and review statuses as at the end of the previous chapter; this file version is enabled for use in Adobe Reader.
- TravelASIA4.pdf is the project complete with comments and review statuses as at the end of the previous chapter, and the enabling feature is removed.
- TravelASIA5.pdf is the project complete with comments, review statuses, and edits described in this chapter.
- TravelASIA_5vs4.pdf is the comparison report on the project file before and after edits.

looking for all comments types p. 92

- Ideally, reviewers will use the correct type of comment for a specific job; for example, text that needs to be replaced should be indicated by a Replace Text Edit comment. In real life, however, it's just as likely that reviewers will indicate a change they'd like to make by using a circle, a highlight, or a note comment. If you sort by comment type to find Text Edit comments for revisions, you may miss a number of other types of edits. To be safe, read through all the comments and use a check mark process to keep track of your work. Over time, as your reviewing expertise develops, you will develop a system that works for your group.

exporting comments for editing p. 93

- The Text Edit comments used in the project are designed for exporting to Word, so if you have the right software, you can try on your own.
- The source Word file for our project is available from the book's Web site, named TravelASIA.doc. You can also download bonus instructions to learn how to export comments to the source Word document. The export process works only in Windows.

extra bits

other ways to make text touchups p. 96

- The method used in our project is the simplest way to replace text that requires changing lines. You can also try simply deleting extra spaces and moving text to previous lines.

- In the example shown in the project, if you delete the spaces outright the rest of the content on the pages shifts upward. If you then press Enter/Return to move the last word to a separate line, not only does the layout not shuffle back to its original positions, but you also have differences in how the text is spaced vertically on the third line. Cutting/pasting prevents shuffling text to get the page back to its original layout.

09 Tots in Thailand: ~~Trading in backpacks for diaper bags—read about one fam~~ily's
adventures.

where did the comments go? p. 99

- You may find on occasion that the visible comment marks such as highlights or crossout lines on the page are moved. This happens when you make adjustments to text and other content on the page using the TouchUp tools.

- You can usually figure out which comment is which. If you can't, open the master copy of the file and check out the comment's exact location—another good reason for using a copy of the file for revisions.

more types of comparisons p. 103

- If you are working with several versions of a document containing different review cycles, it is a good idea to make a comparison to see whether you are working with the newest version of a file, for example, or that your changes have been made.

- In our project, we compared documents based on textual differences, as all our changes except one were made to text. You could also select Page By Page Visual Differences as a comparison option, and specify the level of detail and highlight color.

- We also chose the Consolidated Report, which adds markups to the current document. You could instead choose to create a Side By Side Report that produces a new PDF file comparing the two documents on side-by-side pages.

index

index

conversion settings (continued)
    commonly used, 15
    shared, 15
Convert to PDF option, 9
Create PDF from Multiple
    Documents dialog, 11, 13
Create PDF of Comments
    Summary option, 87
Create PDF Task button, 11
creating PDF files, 7–16
    checking text files before, 8
    conversion settings for, 9–10,
      15
    general overview of, 7
    source programs and, 16
    steps in process of, 11–14
Cross Out Text for Deletion
    option, 41
customizing review options, 21

D

default comments, 50
Distribution List, 26
docking toolbars, 31
Document Message Bar, 29, 35
Document pane, 2
Document Status icon, 35, 43
document versions, 103–104
downloading project files, 15
Drawing Markups toolbar, 29,
    31, 46
Drawing tools, 47
drawings as comments, 47
dynamic stamp, 44

E

edit comments. See Text Edit
    comments
editing PDF files, 89–106
    arranging the window, 95

comparing versions,
    103–104, 106
    image touchups, 101–102
    listing comments, 93–94
    organizing revisions, 92
    saving files before, 90–91
    text touchups, 96–98
    tracking progress of, 99–100
email
    receiving comments via,
      54–55
    returning comments via,
      48, 52
    sending reviews by, 18,
      19, 25
embedded fonts, 8
enabling PDF files, 26, 27
exporting comments, 81–82,
    87, 105

F

FDF files, 37, 52
File Attachment Properties
    dialog, 43
file comments, 43
File toolbar, 2
filtering comments, 61–62,
    63, 75
fonts, embedded, 8

G

General Preferences, 6
grammar check, 8
grouping comments, 79, 87
guides, 101, 102

H

Hand tool, 42, 101
Help topics, 34

hiding prompts, 25
High Quality print settings, 15
highlight comments, 51
History feature, 25
How To window, 3, 30
    showing and hiding, 36
    using in Adobe Reader, 33–34

I

icons
    for comments, 40, 50, 59
    for special features, 6
identity, comment, 49
Identity panel, 25
image touchups, 101–102
Import Comments dialog, 57
importing comment files, 56–57,
    63
Indicate Text Edits Tool, 41, 42
initiator of reviews, 17, 27, 53
"insert text" icon, 50
invitations, review, 20, 22–23

J

joboptions files, 7

K

keyboard shortcuts, 6

L

Launch Attachment dialog, 51
layers icon, 6
locked comments, 104
locked toolbars, 5

index